BY SIMON RAVEN

The Feathers of Death

Brother Cain

Doctors Wear Scarlet

The Decline
of the
Gentleman

SIMON RAVEN

Simon and Schuster • New York • 1962

Library of Congress Catalog Card Number: 62-7556
Manufactured in the United States of America
By American Book-Stratford Press, Inc., New York, N. Y.

Drake he's in his hammock till the great Armadas come,
　(Capten, art tha sleepin' there below?)
Slung atween the round shot, listenin' for the drum,
　An' dreamin' arl the time o' Plymouth Hoe. . . .
　　　　　　　　—SIR HENRY NEWBOLT, *Drake's Drum*

He despised the mean arts and unreasonable clamours of
demagogues. He despised still more the doctrines of divine
right and passive obedience.
　　　　　　　—LORD MACAULAY, *History of England*, Ch. ii

CONTENTS

APOLOGY

I MYSELF AM NOT a gentleman. If I were, I would almost certainly not be writing this book, for one of the marks of a gentleman is that he seldom mentions the question of gentility, whether in application to others or to himself. There are a number of reasons why I am not a gentleman, some of which will become abundantly plain in the following pages; but chief among them is that I have no sense of obligation. I am happy to enjoy privilege; I am also prone to evade or even totally to ignore its implicit commitments. This defect would not necessarily disqualify me from being "upper-class," but it does mean that I can never be a gentleman, which is a very different thing.

As it happens, I am not "upper-class" either. The reasons for this range from middle-class parentage, through chronic and perpetual lack of ready money, to a sneaking fondness for baked beans on toast at tea time. But somewhere among them lurks the most powerful reason of all—guilt. For although I am prepared to arrogate privilege and disown obligation (in itself a very upper-class way of behaving), I always feel guilty about so doing. This is not to say I make any attempt to mend my ways—I am much too fond of comfort for that—but it does mean that I am uneasy about the advantages which I receive and so cannot enjoy them with the full relish and assurance proper to an uncompromising member of the upper class. Thus I have the worst of both worlds. Exiled forever from the courts of gentility by a kind of ingrowing dishonor, I am yet ineligible to play the shameless aristocrat, even when I have the means, because I am sadly conscious of that dishonor and so must always be making groveling gestures to allay my guilt. For example,

I always overtip; not out of generosity, which would be all right, nor even out of a desire to show off, which would be tolerable, but because deep down inside me I am afraid that the waiter has in fact detected my vileness and may, unless heavily bribed to refrain, at any moment turn and rend me for it.

There are, of course, consolations. Belonging to neither party, I need be loyal to neither. On the one hand, being known to be no gentleman, I am not blamed by my acquaintance when I behave like a cad, maltreating a woman or failing to return a loan; it is what is expected of me and is received with equanimity by all. On the other hand, since I am known to lack the steely self-sufficiency, the boundless ability to overlook the feelings or welfare of others, that is perhaps the purest characteristic of the upper class, no one is disposed to mock me for some pitiful display of bourgeois weakness, like apologizing to the restaurateur if a member of my party has been sick on him. My upper-class acquaintance simply recognize my lack of assurance, and then deprecate but tolerate my condition.

Still, you see my problem. I should like to be a gentleman, or, alternatively, I should adore to be a member of the upper class: both aspirations are entirely vain. After long thought, however, it has become clear to me that it is possible, if not to alter, at least to rationalize my predicament by demonstrating that it is nowadays irrelevant and almost out of the question *to be a gentleman at all,* and that such gentlemen as survive, though honorable and decent men, can only be seen as futile anachronisms when once one properly appreciates the present conditions of society. The mere member of the upper class, as distinct from the gentleman, needs no further castigation these days; we all know how disgraceful *he* is. But the gentleman still retains, in some quarters at least, a title to respect, and he is still, therefore, a worthwhile target of attack. It is thought that he behaves well, is dutiful and responsible, accepts only so much in the way of privilege as his dignity and office strictly necessitate, and would not dream of exploiting or boasting about such superior talents as he may possess—this last a great comfort to the envious and the democratically minded. It is also averred that, as his name implies, he is "gentle," *i.e.* mild, in his dealings. The last conception, as it happens, is based on a misunderstanding of the adjective "gentle" (Latin: *gentilis*), which in this context simply means "worthy or typical of a kind (or *genus*)" and has nothing to do with meekness. But this misunderstanding, by its very existence, only pays further tribute to the good character of the gentleman. The gentleman, then, unlike the already discredited aristocrat, is fair game. He still has a name to lose; and it is the purpose of this book to take that name justly and finally from him.

I have owned that my motives are partly those of wounded *amour propre*—someone else would have said so if I hadn't. But even so, my pique is not directed so much at surviving gentlemen *in ipsis* as at the state of affairs which has rendered them incongruous in survival. For while I am jealous of gentlemen because I am not of their number, I nevertheless admire them deeply and find myself out of sympathy with an age which in essence rejects them. The plain fact remains that *we are of our age,* and that this age, properly understood, has no use and no regard for gentility. And so, while this book may have had its origins in personal frustration, its arguments have some claim to balance: If I resent the gentleman, I am no friend to his common detractor; and in dealing with either of them I have made some effort to eschew prejudice and to argue from the observed social facts of our time.

Anyone who writes about society should first place himself in relation to society. So far I have only done this in a very general way; here are some of the more relevant details.

I was born in 1927 in a nursing home in Welbeck Street; and as this venue implies, my parents were well-to-do. My father was the son of a self-made industrialist whose factory and effects, being turned into ready money after his death, had realized close on a million pounds, which was then divided equally between the ten-odd children of his two marriages. My mother, coming of a Cambridge family of long-established but only middling tradesmen, had brought no money to her wedding; but my father, though he did no work, had quite enough to support a family in solid comfort. Thus on one side I was two generations out of the gutter, while on the other I had a petty bourgeois inheritance of at least a hundred years. I grew up in Surrey stockbrokers' country, was sent to a smartish Surrey prep school (sixty guineas a term—a high fee before the war), was evacuated in 1940 to a competent and rather cheaper school in Somerset, and in 1941 won top scholarship to Charterhouse. Hence I was expelled for homosexuality in the autumn of 1945, but not before I had won a Classical Scholarship to King's College, Cambridge, and played in the same school cricket XI as Peter May. There followed a happy time in the rough and ready Army of the immediately postwar period. Since the war was too recently concluded for people to worry much about morality, my disgrace at Charterhouse did not prevent my being sent to India as a Cadet and then duly sent back again with a commission in the Oxfordshire and Buckinghamshire Light Infantry, a regiment of sound if hardly brilliant social standing. I was consequently forgiven by the authorities at Charterhouse and allowed to join the old boys' association. Meanwhile King's College, in its benign traditional tolerance, had never made much of my expulsion and indeed by this time had probably forgotten all about it; so I was allowed to come up to Cambridge, after being demobilized in 1948, with the privileges and emoluments of a Foundation Scholar and with the boundless anticipation of pleasure and enlightenment proper to my extreme youth.

Of King's I shall have more to say later in this book. Enough to remark here that my expectations were little disappointed, but that I repaid the kind attentions I received by getting dangerously into debt and badly confounding my tutor's hopes in my final Tripos. Even so, I was elected to a Studentship so that I could stay on at the College and write a thesis in competition for a Fellowship. To this piece of consideration, for which I was genuinely grateful, I responded by getting even deeper into debt and totally neglecting my research. For I had begun to have outside aspirations; I was being allowed to write reviews for a well-known weekly, I had written a novel of which I thought highly (it never appeared, I am thankful to record), and the anonymous routine of low-paid and conscientious research sorted ill with my new character of cosmo-

politan literateur. As Cyril Connolly has it, I required to be paid—
and still more important, praised—on the nail. I had my deserts: a
little cash, a little praise—and the total collapse of my hopes of a
Fellowship, which I had foolishly seen as something one might
dawdle into with the insouciant idleness of a latter-day Petronius.
Being disabused of this illusion, I saw it was time to go. King's College and I had had enough of each other for the time being. But go
where?

I then took one of the few decisions I have never regretted. It
was at that time very easy for any graduate who had previously held
a temporary commission to return to the Army, with a regular commission and back-dated seniority, after completing his university
course. After four years at Cambridge this seemed just the thing.
Travel, action, a breath of fresh air. . . . My application was accepted, and within a few months of deserting my research I found
myself a senior lieutenant in the King's Shropshire Light Infantry.
Of this excellent corps, as of King's College, I shall have more to
say later. For the present I shall only say that by my regiment, as
by my college, I was treated with every kindness and given every
opportunity—treatment to which I reacted, after some four and a
half years, by becoming so deeply indebted to so many bookmakers
that I was assured of total ruin. At this juncture my seniors, so far
from showing ill will, used all their influence to speed my resignation through what are normally very cumbrous processes, it being
their wish to get me safely out of the Army before the scandal became so openly obtrusive as to require official action—which in this
case would have meant my trial by court-martial for conduct un-
becoming the character of an officer and a gentleman. Their efforts
were successful: the Army Council's acceptance of my resignation
reached the regimental headquarters a few days before the first of
the bookmakers' emissaries, and I was therefore free, as a private
person, to repudiate my debts without any punishment more severe
than being warned off the Turf.

And so, at the age of thirty, I had successively disgraced myself
with three fine institutions, each of which had made me free of its
full and rich resources, had trained me with skill and patience, and

had shown me nothing but forbearance and charity when I failed in trust. Small wonder I was becoming a prey to guilt. Small wonder I was beginning to realize that, whatever else I might become, I was now discredited far beyond the point where I could claim to be a gentleman. True, my defects were negative, consisting in vanity and weakness rather than in active malice. Even so . . . But there were now other and more pressing considerations. For one thing, I had to eat. Money must be procured, some sort of career contrived. I must clearly take up again the literary connections which had made me so vain of myself while still at Cambridge. For in a literary career there was one unfailing advantage: No degree whatever of moral or social disgrace could disqualify one from practice—and indeed a bad character, if suitably tricked out for presentation, might win one helpful publicity. It wouldn't even matter if one went to prison. The abdication was final; by becoming a writer one bade farewell at once to ethical restraint and to any kind of conventional status in society.

In all fairness to myself, I should add that I did have a modest talent for the pursuit of letters. I enjoyed writing, and it was my pride to render clear and enjoyable what I wrote. A reader, I thought, must pay in time and in money for his reading; both courtesy and equity therefore required, not indeed that one should defer to his possible opinions, but that one should attempt to entertain him while demonstrating one's own. This is a matter of the simplest common sense, but as relatively few aspirant writers ever seem to grasp the point, those that do set out with a distinct advantage. But let all this be as it may, my fortune has been moderately kind in the three years since I "resigned" from the Army and commenced properly as author. I am allowed to write reviews and even long essays for certain established periodicals; and I have, up to this time, published three novels, one of which at least has been kindly received.

Now, I have given this potted autobiography in order to let the reader know where I stand. In the same way as it was only fair to confess to some personal pique at being neither a gentleman nor a member of the upper class myself, similarly it is but proper that I should present other and more detailed circumstances of my life, so that anyone who wishes may count the chips on my shoulder and then discount what follows in this book to allow for such prejudices as he may think my career and background have induced in me. For my part, I can only say that I have attempted to see to my prejudices myself; and I should also like to point out that of the three institutions—school, college and regiment—that have in various degrees and with good reason rejected me, for none do I feel *personally* anything save the warmest affection, whatever criticisms I may offer on other levels. Finally, it should be clear from the foregoing account that I am qualified to write of those whom society calls "gentlemen" in this respect at least—that I have, after all, passed most of my life in their company.

It now remains, since this apologia is also an introduction, that I should say something more of the thesis of this book—should give broad notice of its argument and division.

In Part One, which I shall call "Tradition," I shall attempt to assemble and discuss the principal elements, cultural, historical and social, which I believe have gone to form the traditional English notion of what constitutes a "gentleman." These separate elements, some of which have been imported from distant races and ages, some of which are truly indigenous, will be seen, for all their diversity, to combine into a coherent and consistent whole. I shall demonstrate this fusion and conclude Part One with a generalized portrait of the English gentleman—his manners, morals, origins, occupations, code of honor and beliefs—as he might have been seen at the beginning of this century and can still, in rare cases, be seen today. I shall also be at some pains to distinguish between those who are gentlemen in the full and demanding sense of the word and those who, through accidents of birth, office, appearance or property, are loosely referred to as such although they have few of the real qualifications. For while there is a certain social level below which no one can properly call himself a gentleman, this level lies quite low in the scale (just how low I shall try to make plain); and I cannot overemphasize that to be a gentleman it is not sufficient, and is not indeed even necessary, to belong to what is known as the "upper class," itself to be investigated more closely later on.

In Part Two, "Degeneration," I shall show how the ideal presented in Part One has either declined or become obsolete during the last fifty years. As a start, we shall go back to the upper class, define it more exactly, and show that the tendency of its members is to rely on externals, such as prestige, power, rank, money or privilege, whereas the gentleman, whether or not he also belongs to the upper class, has always been more concerned with justice, obligation and duty. I shall then point out that there has been in this country for some time an increasing popular concern with overt status and material goods, that the main social emphases are now fixed in such things, and that in consequence men are judged largely in relation to them. From which it follows that a man's quality is far more likely to be assessed, not with reference to his character, courage and probity, but in accordance with such upper-class criteria as "pounds sterling and strawberry leaves." To make matters worse, such standards are applied in the most vulgar and philistine fashion. After all, one might tolerate a world in which a man was revered as a relative of the King or for his collection of antique statuary, but it is not easy to acquiesce when prestige is conferred by the ownership of a Bentley or an expensive greyhound.

We shall then consider, since it is closely linked with the above phenomenon, the contemporary *distrust of personal excellence*. On the whole, people do not resent other people's possessions, if only because they might at any time "come up on the pools" themselves; but what *does* stir up jealousy and ill feeling is the idea that someone might be, *in himself and for his own qualities,* superior to the general run. Now, this type of excellence demanded of a gentleman is very limited; but excellence it nevertheless remains, particularly in matters of character and conduct. The average man will no longer suffer that someone else should appear superior on this or any other personal ground, and so one way of settling things is for *everyone* to announce that he is a gentleman. Since the necessary integrity and sense of honor can hardly be assimilated overnight, recourse is had to externals. One man has been a temporary officer during the war and now joins the territorials for the prestige of the commission; another can just manage a B.B.C. accent; a third has a habit of dress or drinking which he considers elegant; a fourth runs a tired hack in the local Point-to-Point. Thus face is saved; by aping the gentleman in one external respect—however trivial—every Jack is made a gentleman, and, once more, we are all equal. After all, everybody nowadays is addressed as "Esq." on his letters and goes through a door marked "Gents."

And so we shall have seen how the general adoption of material standards and the general resentment at personal quality have combined to cheapen the notion of gentility. But the case is even worse. For the trouble is that even if a man admires the true ideal of gentility and wishes to conform to its canons, he will find that it is now either impossible or irrelevant to do so. It has always, for example, been the mark of a gentleman to lend public support to the established religion of his country—however strong his private doubts. But if ever there was an irrelevance in English life, it has been, since 1918, the Church of England. Or again, a gentleman recognizes his obligations to those less fortunately placed—all of which obligations have now been firmly shouldered by the State. Good manners will more likely prove an embarrassment than an asset: Offer your seat in the tube to a woman or an older man, and some young lout will probably crash down on it while you are still being thanked. (This has happened in my presence twice in the last three months.) To be grave on a grave occasion is to be seen as "pompous"; discipline is viewed either as "provocation" or "thwarting of personality"; the display of courage as "what we'd *all* have done if we'd been there." Let me labor the point no further: The ideal of gentility has widely declined, and those who are still true to the banner will find themselves the victims either of mockery, envy or indifference, and in no case able to render the services they wish.

So far the discussion will have been largely theoretical. In Part Three, "Illustration," I propose to offer concrete evidence for my thesis. It will be the longest section of the book but needs only a short description here. I intend, quite simply, to give accounts of certain people and circumstances in my own life. I shall describe how I was trained, at school, to adopt the correct gentlemanly ethic, how I betrayed this ethic, but how I have since seen the ethic itself, rendered futile by the times, betray those who were true to it. I shall give an account of some of the "upper-class" cavortings which I have witnessed in London and elsewhere—concrete instances of the decay of manners and morals which has perverted public taste and brought disrepute on an imperial class. I shall also tell of some gentlemen I knew in the Army—how they were still able, in the artificial conditions which prevailed, to assert themselves usefully under arms, and how they were ruthlessly beaten down when, for one reason or another, they emerged into the outer world. Finally, I shall say something of my time at King's College, Cambridge; my purpose in this being to show that tolerance, learning and skepticism, the paramount virtues of the place, may inculcate an ethic which, flexible yet not dishonorable, will equip a man to deal with present realities in a practical but seemly fashion that cannot be taught by the defunct codes of gentility. I am sorry that the gentleman has passed; after telling the manner of his passing, I shall be at some pains (though I expect no thanks for them) to suggest how we may fill his place.

PART ONE

Tradition

Hic manus ob patriam pugnando volnera passi,
quique sacerdotes casti, dum vita manebat,
quique pii vates et Phoebo digna locuti,
inventas aut qui vitam excoluere per artis,
quique suit memores aliquos fecere merendo . . .
  —VIRGIL, *Aeneid,* Book VI: ll. 660—664

SWEET REASON

THROUGHOUT HISTORY, numberless different ideals of social behavior have prevailed. Those few that have proved, for whatever reasons, sympathetic to Englishmen have sooner or later been incorporated into the English tradition of gentility. In the following chapters I shall give a brief account of the most important of such ideals; and in this chapter I shall start with those learned from the Greeks, not because they were the first to influence Englishmen, but because it was only as they gradually seeped through to our island that we ceased to be savages (albeit quite rich and well-organized ones) and became civilized men and women.

It is important to grasp from the outset that what sanctimonious schoolmasters have said in their generations of the ancient Greeks would not necessarily have been endorsed by the Greeks themselves. For various reasons—mainly those of warped morality and misapplied tact—the pedagogue has found it convenient to suppress some things and exaggerate others. But while the picture that has emerged is no doubt misleading, it is equally important to grasp that it is the pedagogue's picture, however shaky its perspective, that has mainly influenced the educated Englishman. He had his Greek on the school bench at an impressionable age; and even if those few of his contemporaries that thought for themselves later questioned what they learned there, the lessons absorbed in extreme youth can never be altogether cut away from the soul. So the average Englishman's Greece, if not exactly that of Dr. Syntax, is never likely to advance far from that of Dr. Arnold. But since, when all is said, Dr. Arnold has graciously permitted a great deal of what is best to survive, we can examine this residue without, at any rate, excessive shame.

The impression which results is something like this.

"The original inhabitants of Greece and her islands, being southern in origin, were a people of passion, pleasure and imagination; fortunately for them, my dear boys, they were conquered at an early stage by some altogether more well-conducted peoples from the north (northerners are always more responsible, remember), and restraint was imposed upon them before things had gone too far. So Greek fire was set to burn in a carefully guarded hearth. The marriage (to change the metaphor, boys) was a success. The northerners did not care much about Art, of course, and they soon put an end to extravagance in *that*; but after a time they allowed it to go on again in a sober and well-controlled way. They also insisted on proper moral standards, although, as you may discover when you grow older, they did not really insist quite *enough*. But perhaps the best thing they did was to direct Greek high spirits into channels of intellectual inquiry. One can easily overdo that kind of thing, but the original southerners had positively underdone it, probably because, as I have already explained, they thought too much about pleasure. But once the people from the north had settled in, southern imaginations were set to work under discipline and supervision, and the result of all this was *reasoned speculation*.

"Now, boys, too much cleverness is not a good thing (never forget that the Greeks came to a *bad end*), and we should seldom inquire further when older and more sensible people have already given us their opinions. But the Greeks had every excuse for curiosity, because they could not, of course, know about Christianity, and the only guide they had was a lot of primitive and unsuitable myths. So in the circumstances they were quite right to seek for the truth themselves. And they sought for it wih energy and passion. I cannot say that they arrived at a consistent body of philosophical conclusion (though lots of them, especially Plato, decided that there was only one God); but in the course of their inquiries they found out a great deal about man and morality and government (not very much about science until Aristotle, who was rather late), and so they were able to reach some valuable opinions and formulate some sound provisional rules for the business of life.

"Here are the most important of them:

"First, the truth must be sought honestly and with intelligence on every level, and must be prized above convenience and even perhaps above freedom itself, because it is not made by man but exists independently of him. It is above man; knowledge of it therefore ennobles man, and, although it is regarded only by the unworthy as something to be exploited (the Greeks, unlike the Romans, despised applied science), its conquest will better man's condition because, giving him some form of certainty in a shifting universe, it will satisfy his soul.

"One comes at the truth by logic, patience and fairmindedness. From which it follows, by extension, that one should always be *moderate*—in the affairs of the mind as in those of the body. This is not to deprecate effort, but it is to say that one should not follow the dictates of blind enthusiasm: One must always pause for thought. The Greeks were well aware of their passionate natures and were therefore aware how easily they could be both mentally and physically seduced; moderation was the weapon prudently forged to protect their virtue. But while I commend this quality to all of you, I am not for one moment condoning slackness. You are not to think that 'moderation' allows you to pause for thought or seek excuse before doing things which you know very well to be duties, like *playing hard* or going to church on Sunday. The Greeks were a fine people, but they were pagans and—er—foreigners, and your parents and teachers know better than they did in many vital respects.

"With moderation comes tolerance, which means that you must always make allowance for the opinions, the arguments and even the shortcomings of other people. But while this is clearly an aid to intellectual and social co-operation, it is not an excuse for conniving at corruption and immoral behavior—as some distinguished humanists would have us think. Christian charity requires that you should pity the evildoer, but also that you should mend his ways for him, and doubtless the Greeks would have agreed with me if they had

had the good fortune to listen to Christ. (What was that? 'To the Greeks foolishness.' did you say? We'll see who looks foolish after class.) To resume, then: Tolerance means respecting the suggestions and opinions of others, but it does not mean that you should fail to report other boys for having dirty thoughts.

"As a result of what I have been telling you, the Greeks, or most of them, thought very much about freedom. They did not like being interfered with by other countries or even other Greek states, and inside their states everyone who was not a slave was very conscious of his 'free' status. Being free meant that you were not *'servile,'* *i.e.*, that subject to the general good you did not have to do anything against your will and must not, as a point of honor, do anything for monetary gain. Nor could you be a place hunter—the Greeks would have had little time for most politicians currently sitting in Parliament, whom they would have considered both timorous and venal. You might, of course, aspire to high place in order to help your people, but not in order to gratify yourself with power or its ornaments. In other words, you should speak your mind without regard to popular prejudice or superstition, fulfill your obligations, and hold yourself wary of privilege. All this has been well put by the Athenian leader Pericles, whose untimely death we may regret without condoning the indulgence of his private life. In public, at least, he expressed stern views about women: They should be heard of, he said, neither for good nor ill. If you think this a little harsh, remember what we endure from Dr. Summerskill or Lady Lewisham, and then think again.

"Finally, I should tell you that the Greeks strongly disapproved of inflated pride, which they called ὕβρις. This, of course, is another very important part of being moderate. They took the view that anyone who became too pleased with himself or thought himself too clever would be punished by the gods with disgrace and ruin, and they wrote a number of strongly worded plays to stress the point. Nowadays we know that this does not always happen: Hitler was punished but Franco hasn't been, and we don't yet know what will happen in marginal cases, like Lord Beaverbrook or Field-Marshal Montgomery. Still, as a general rule, especially for small boys, it is a very good one. Pride goes before a fall—as some of us will now find out. You may all go except the boy—Connolly again?—who made that remark about 'to the Greeks foolishness.' Whatever the Athenians might have thought, we do not allow the devil to quote scripture *here. . ."*

This kind of lesson, despite its many omissions and false emphases, has conveyed to generations of English boys a tolerable idea of the Greek achievement. Controlled passion for truth, a certain flexibility in human affairs, a concern for freedom, honor and the public good without too much thought of personal reward . . . all this in the end comes through. So that myriad fourteen-year-olds must have concluded, and they could have come to far worse conclusions, that the Greeks stood for finding and facing facts, keeping cool, and playing fair.

2

PIETAS

IF EVER THERE WAS a dreary way of describing an epic hero, it seems at first sight to be Virgil's constant qualification of Aeneas as *"pius."* The Trojan leader, despite his versatility and courage, is at best wooden and at worst a downright prig; and when one is reminded, even in the pit of Hades or at the end of a violent lovers' quarrel, that it is the *"pius Aeneas"* who is featuring in all this, one can only conclude that Fate had made a feeble choice and that widow Dido was well rid of him.

But while no amount of admiration for Virgil can persuade one to see his Aeneas save as an artistic blunder and a catastrophic bore, to deride this hero for his *pietas,* as though it made of him a kind of Lord's Day Observance nark, is to miss an important point. The word "pious" has long since decayed in the English language and is now applied only to those who combine self-satisfaction with the meaner virtues. At its best, however, "pious" meant something very different; and as for *pius*, it conveyed to Virgil and his contemporaries a central notion of high dignity and national significance. It meant nothing less than that a man was faithful, loyal and true, first to his country and its institutions (among which came the country's gods), and secondly to his ancestors and his kin. By styling Aeneas *pius* Virgil was not suggesting that he was a chaste teetotal goody-goody but was reminding us that, in obedience to the gods and among them his mother Venus, he was leading his people to win their promised inheritance in the West.

Thus the Roman concept of *pietas* had little to do with individual salvation; it was a fundamental ideal of social behavior. It represented a man's inalienable duty to honor his father and mother, preserve the house which had been built by his ancestors, pay homage to the ancient gods of Rome, and pay equal homage to the institutions which gods and ancestors had together devised for their own lasting glory and his temporary benefit. It was a conservative ideal, inculcating courage, temperance and something more than respect for the established way of life, and, demanding strict discipline, it promised in return increase and good order. It resulted in a practical ethic as cruel as it was honorable, for to depart from it meant death for oneself and ruin for all one's dependants.

Closely allied with *pietas* were *gravitas* and *dignitas*. *Gravitas* (*gravis*, heavy) meant the weightiness or proper weight of a thing or, metaphorically, of an idea, law or tradition, and so, by an easy transference, the moral weight of those chosen to attend to such weighty matters. "Most potent, grave and reverend," the Venetian elders had *gravitas*. They were serious about serious things, fit men to shoulder a heavy moral burden.

Dignitas can be translated as worthiness. Since this at first seems a neutral expression, its imputation might theoretically depend on circumstance (thus a display of *dignitas*—worthiness of the surroundings—would not be edifying in a brothel), but like many such neutral words (*e.g.*, kindly, natural) it came to be used only for good. A man had *dignitas* if he conducted himself worthily among great men and on great occasions. Then, by extension, his *dignitas* remained even when the company or conditions deteriorated; he would behave worthily of his high office and acquaintance even when thrown into a mean assembly. Thus *dignitas* no longer depends on the surroundings but on the man, and will enable him to emerge with grace from the most squalid situation.

Dignitas, then, can be seen as the outward accompaniment of *gravitas.* Grave thoughts lead to dignified comportment. Throw in *pietas* as well, and the combination is formidable. So were the Romans. But surely, it will be urged, there was a certain falling off. The Divine Julius showed rather too much flexibility, to put it mildly, and by the time we get to the Divine Nero . . . true, true. But remember, gentle reader, that the young are instructed in the massive virtues of the Republic rather than in the engaging decadence of the Empire. And remember too that for every boy who learns about the Greeks, five learn about the Romans. Their lessons tell them that the Romans raised a mere hill-village to eternal greatness by being serious about serious issues, keeping straight faces, honoring their patriotic and family obligations, and by being loyal to the gods and to one another.

3

SWORDS AND PLOWSHARES

IT HAS ALWAYS BEEN possible to attain to gentility by skill at arms. Obversely, a gentleman has always been required to justify his position by military service.

The simplest introduction to this aspect of the matter is to consider elementary feudal procedures. In the first place, then, let us take a landless man who has offered his military services to a lord to whom, hitherto, he has owed no obligation. He would be sworn into vassalage for the duration of the pending campaign and would then be ranked in accordance with his equipment. If he had a horse and rough armor, then he would rank as a lesser knight. If his armor was rather more elaborate, then he might rank as a greater knight, claiming low precedence among the landed barons and the knights who had brought followers from their estates. But the position of the landless man was always precarious. People would want to know how he came by his horse and armor in the first place, these being items of enormous cost, and if he could not point to some influential relative or put up a good story of having won them earlier in battle, he would be suspected of having stolen them. Equally, since his position was held by virtue of his equipment, should his horse die and not be replaceable he would have to serve among the footmen or engage himself as esquire to someone better placed. In either case his armor would still procure him consideration, but his prospects of advancement would now be very much dimmer unless and until he could beg, borrow, or win another horse.

If fortune were kind, on the other hand, our landless man might be noticed for his courage and energy and perhaps be given a small command of infantry or even of other knights. Or he might be installed in a stronghold or castle, in which case, in return for holding it for his lord, he might even be granted permanent tenure and would thus have the nucleus of future power and estate. Similarly, if he survived honorably to the end of a successful campaign, he might then be rewarded with broad lands and high office under his lord, either in conquered territory or even back in the lord's own domains. But whatever the outcome, two things are plain: There were glittering prizes for glittering swords to win, and, secondly and more to our present purpose, a man automatically had gentle or knightly status if he could present himself and a sufficiency of arms in readiness to do battle.

By contrast, let us consider the man who was already settled in possession of estates. These he would either hold of the King, or of the Church, or of a greater nobleman. He almost certainly held them as reward for his own or his ancestors' services; and he was still under obligation, in return for the right of tenure, to fight for his overlord if required and to bring with him men under his banner who corresponded in number and accouterment to the width and wealth of his holdings. Thus the situation of the landless adventurer is reversed: The latter set out to claim rank by virtue of arms and to win higher rank by his prowess; but the acknowledged landholder must confirm his rank by royalty and a good showing of followers, under pain of being dispossessed for defaulting from his obligations and so breaking his oath.

At this stage, it is easy to discern a pattern. Service under arms procures, from King, Church or Nobility, one's recognition as a man of gentle or knightly quality. King, Church or Nobility are also obliged, in return for an oath of loyalty, to protect one as a vassal and to reward one, preferably with land, for outstanding service. Once one is thus requited, not only does one's oath still stand but one must do yet more to meet it: As a tenant of land, one must bring followers if required, and one therefore displays a banner to rally them and is now known as a knight banneret. (This despite the fact that one will probably *fight* as one of a unit of cavalry, *i.e.* among other knights, while one's men will be dispatched, in case of battle, to serve under a captain of foot.) All the time, one is conscious of *obligation*, one's own to serve one's lord and protect one's followers, the lord's to protect oneself and obey *his* feudal superior in turn. The pattern, in short, is simply one of reciprocal obligation as enforced by oath and made tolerable (for the more fortunate) by reward and privilege.

It is here that we have the root both of honor and of rank, which together must detain us for some time. As for honor, there were of course further complications. Apart from one's feudal oath, there was an elaborate code of knightly conduct (also enforced by oath) which decreed, among other things, mercy to the weak, respect for women and unfailing loyalty to the Church—as a spiritual authority, in this case, and quite apart from its local or secular powers. There was also the question of "face." This entailed not only conducting oneself with courage and dignity but being seen and *acknowledged* to have done so. Inevitably, therefore, it implied a duty to hound down and punish one's detractors and, in general, any man who had broken faith with the system. But in the end, whatever the frills and side issues, a knight's honor was based on the fulfillment of contract and *feudal obligation,* an obligation which reached both up and down. Even his loyalty to the Church, as the earthly instrument of the Christian God, can often be seen as the result of a clear if unspoken understanding whereby the Church, in return for his support, gave its spiritual sanction to his temporal or hierarchical claims.

Mention of hierarchy brings us on to the second and more complex question—the scale and detail of social rank. Since it was feudal method and procedure upon which was founded the system of social ranks which survives to this present day, and since it is important that we get this matter absolutely straight, particularly with regard to the title of "gentleman," this will be a suitable juncture at which to settle it.

Initial heraldic inquiries are complicated by the fact that the recurring word "baron" (which in Latin—*baro*—first meant a dunce and then, by a dubious process of extension, an important officer under the later Empire) was indiscriminately used of any substantial landholder. As time went on, however, and as the King took to summoning his nobles to Parliament by writs specifying their degree, it became clear that baron was the lowest rank among the *nobiles maiores,* which is to say the nobility proper or Peers of Parliament as opposed to the *nobiles minores,* a term comprehending knights banneret, knights, esquires and gentlemen—in one word, the gentry. Under the Royal Family, then, from a duke down to a baron you were noble, from a knight banneret down to a mere gentleman you were gentle. If, in the light of this we consider once more the military camp at which our original landless man presented himself, it is easy to see how rank within the gentry corresponded to function. The knight banneret, while not noble, was a landholder who had brought men, probably very few, under his own banner. The knight was a properly armed and trained horseman who came without following. The esquire (Latin *scutarius,* or shield bearer) —was the honored attendant of an important knight or nobleman—

possibly his son—who aspired to knighthood but was either too poor in armor or simply too young yet to be granted the dignity. The gentleman was one who, making a living by his sword, was relatively well armed but unmounted; and he ranked above the common foot soldier or pressed vassal for one or all of the following reasons: First, and essentially, because of his superior training and accouterment; secondly because, while not honored with a place as esquire, he might well come of a known family; and thirdly perhaps because, though hitherto under no feudal obligation to his commander, he had voluntarily taken an oath of allegiance. He might or might not be given a command of foot; if not, he would fight as one of the "heavy" infantry; and readers of *Henry V* will doubtless remember that that monarch, whilst incognito on the eve of Agincourt, thought fit to announce himself as "a gentleman of a company." In any event whatever, his status entitled him, like a knight or esquire, to look for lands and advancement if things went well— rewards seldom bestowed on pressed vassals or base hired footmen.

Now, to our ears it sounds absurd that a man capable of producing a mere platoon of men in the field should rank as a superior knight, and still more absurd that a heavily armed foot soldier should have the status of gentleman. The whole system seems inflated. But I should point out that society has always paid disproportionate honor to its soldiers, particularly in ages when violence was a commonplace and protectors desirable. We are now talking of such an age—an age, moreover, in which properly armed troops were extremely hard to come by in any number. I should add that even well into the eighteenth century the Life Guards were manned by troopers of education and sound family (among them Mr. Addison and Mr. Steele) who, while serving in the ranks as private men, were nevertheless accorded the title of gentlemen and much of the respect due to officers and were paid a wage which Macaulay tells us (*History of England*, Ch. III) enabled them to live in excellent style. Such is the esteem which a soldier, particularly if he be mounted, may command. The blunt truth is that primitive peoples start, for obvious reasons, by giving high place to warriors and witch doctors, and that this means of stratification is so firmly ratified by custom and by fear that it later persists, in favor now of the soldier and the priest, as the guiding principle of more advanced social structures. Even today, we hold the feeblest ordinand in some regard, while we decorate successful officers with a munificence that is denied other professional men of comparable parts.

But although we still amuse ourselves by bestowing feudal titles on military men, we have come a long way since the days when our landless man appeared in camp and produced his war horse as evidence of knightly rank. Even quite early in feudal times, as wars became more specialized and the hire of skilled mercenaries more advisable, there was a shift, in the higher circles, away from military values and toward those more consistent with the peaceful ownership of land. This shift made for changes in social emphasis and gradation—changes which we can best begin to distinguish by following our once landless man away from camp at the end of a prosperous campaign and on to the estate which has been newly granted him.

Let us postulate for him several years of peace, or assume that he compounds for future military service by sending his overlord money with which to hire independent bands of troops. This enables him to stay put, maintain his lands in good condition, and marry a wife. In due course he has two sons, both of whom he sends as pages to his lord's court, and a daughter, who is kept at home and will be married in time to a neighbor. His elder son, when grown, serves in attendance on his lord during an unimportant campaign, is still too young for knighthood at the end of it, and returns home to assist his now aging father in managing the estate he will inherit. The younger son can see little future as a soldier (the times, after all, are peaceful), and there is no real place for him at home; so he engages himself to a trader to accompany and protect a train of valuable merchandise which is to be sent through France to Italy. As the son of a knight, and having been fully trained at a nobleman's court, he is probably entitled to the degree of esquire; but he finds the expression has little meaning when he has no lord to attend and now that he is no longer in military circles. In his new world of trade he is content to be known simply as a man of "gentle" birth

—a modest pretension which he is able to support in lavish style when, some years later, his grateful employer gives him a permanent place in his company. His sons will receive a "gentle" upbringing; they will not return to their father's background of court and castle, they will not become esquires or knights, but, conscious of sound ancestry and the growing repute of the merchant's calling, they will continue to think of themselves as gentlemen and will so instruct their children.

Meanwhile, the elder brother, late attendant esquire on his father's overlord, has returned home to his father's manor. The years of peace continue, the estate is well tended, justice of a kind dispensed; his father dies, and shortly afterwards he makes some useful money by taking a small share in a trading venture of his brother's company. He continues, like his father, to compound for military service by paying his lord in gold. Such is his prestige, however, and such are his *theoretical* military obligations, that he is almost certain to be thought of as a knight whether or not he has been actually dubbed. At this time, knighthood is still automatically connected with a certain military potential, his manor gives him that potential, and the mere recognition of his overlord, or even of his social equals, may be said to confer the honor of knighthood. But as the years go on, social rank is ever more carefully codified. Our original landless man's great-great-grandson, who is a child when the Wars of the Roses end, finds that he must seek recognition as a knight (should he wish for it) at the King's court in London. Since his father had fought in the late wars and had ended up on the winning side, he might have hoped to assume knighthood as his father's son. But no. He has his fine estate, but the rules governing rank are now far stricter. The eldest son of a knight, until dubbed knight by the king, is now "esquire"; the younger sons are "gentlemen." These latter will go into the world to sink or swim as they may; their elder brother will remain as esquire—or 'squire— of his estate, a title which will be held by his eldest son and so on *in perpetuum*. This title goes not so much with the acres as with the inherited dignity of those that won and kept the right to them by military service. Even at this stage, when the medieval era is fading into the Tudor, the title of esquire has military undertones and the landowner, though no longer a knight by possession, is reckoned, and will continue to be reckoned until our own day, as inheriting a military function—albeit the scope of this becomes increasingly vague with time.

By the accession of the Tudors, then, social rank was beginning to be sensibly regulated (it had always been a subject of attention and dispute), and even a substantial landowner was not necessarily accorded a rank which once went with a suit of armor and a horse. During the next two centuries the hierarchical structure of society became finally firm and its individual ranks were exactly defined. "Society consists," said an eighteenth-century judge, "of noblemen, baronets, knights, esquires, gentlemen, yeomen, tradsmen and artificers." At first sight, apart from the introduction of the seventeenth-century title of baronet, these gradations may seem very similar to those of feudal times; but their meanings, by virtue of the process we have been considering, are now much altered. A baronet or knight is given his title by the King himself and in return for special services or in recognition of eminence—not just for routine military performance. An esquire is the son of a nobleman, the eldest son of a baronet or knight (and his eldest son *in perpetuum*), the eldest son of a nobleman's younger son and his eldest son *in perpetuum*, the holder of certain offices around the King's body or household, the hereditary holder of what was formerly a knight's manor, and a commissioned officer of or above the military rank of captain or the naval equivalent. (Certain legal and academic degrees also confer the dignity.) A gentleman is the younger son of a baronet or knight, the son of an esquire, a commissioned officer below the military rank of captain (or the naval equivalent), and, in general, any man of means or good profession who, while not an esquire, is yet not to be ranked with the yeomen. Having said all this, I will now say my last word as to hierarchical rank: In the narrow or technical sense, "gentleman" is the lowest of the noble and gentle ranks, coming below "esquire" and above "yeoman."

If this seems a miserable mouse to come from such a mountain of labor, I must urge that the inquiry has yielded much useful information by the way. For we have been firmly reminded that gentility has traditionally and almost aboriginally been connected with military office and with the lands held in return for fulfilling such office. It does not do to insist too exclusively on this. As time went on, there was a shift not only from the camp to the manor but also away from the manor itself—to trade, industry or the professions. The way had been well paved by generations of younger sons, and the elder sons of a later age often saw fit to follow them. The plain fact remains that the gentlemen of England have mostly stayed put, for as long as possible, on their land. They have farmed it, hunted over it, delivered justice to those that lived on it; nor have they ever allowed themselves to forget their obligation to fight for it.

For even today it is one of the acknowledged duties of the hereditary landowner to take up commissioned rank in the local Yeomanry or Territorials. True, since the middle of the nineteenth century there has been a growing tendency to serve with the "smart" London regiments—the Guards or the Rifles—in actual time of war. But this applies more to the absentee landlord or to the man who has long since turned his acres into cash; the modest gentleman who is resident on his own property still trains with his tenants in peacetime and fights with them in war—insofar as the complex exigencies of modern armies will permit. For he sees himself, in a sense, as still holding his land of the Sovereign; the Sovereign's quarrels are therefore his quarrels, and he must bring men under his banner to prove his loyalty and love.

Conversely, it is still true that military rank or function confers gentility. If a man who is not a gentleman is commissioned by the Queen, he assumes gentility with his commission. Until very recently commissions were still drawn, in the case of subalterns, specifying the recipient as "our trusty and well beloved A——— B———, gentleman," or, for captains and above, "A——— B———, esquire." To save time and paper, or to avoid upsetting democratic susceptibilities, this is no longer done. But it is still *deemed* to have been done, and every cadet who marches up the college steps at Sandhurst knows that he is now a gentleman, in that he has a technically correct claim to the title if for no other reason. The old rule still holds: It is a gentleman's duty to take an honorable place in battle; and anyone who wins such a place must needs be called a gentleman.

4

CONSCIENCE AND THE KING

WHEN CONSIDERING seventeenth-century England, one does well to bear in mind this prefatory proposition: that the Renaissance had assumed in this island a largely ethical character.

In the broadest terms, the Renaissance in Italy and on the continent as a whole had led to a split between religion and intellect, between the Church and the arts. Intellect said that the earth went round the sun, and His Holiness would have none of it. The arts, newly reawakened to pagan delight in delectable flesh and proportionate form, found the old gods more worthy of representation than the drab or hysterical *personae* of Christian hagiologies; even if a painting were labeled Virgin and Child, it could often be seen more easily as one of Venus and the infant Cupid. The Italian Renaissance had brought Jupiter and his turbulent crew down once more from Olympus, had put Pan back in the forest to taunt St. Francis, and, in its more serious moments, conned the splendid periods of Lucretius and found no place in them for Jehovah.

To England, however, the Renaissance came late and was carried there by careful hands. Stern scholars, caring little for nymphs and godlings, taught the Greek of the New Testament as well as that of Plato. The Renaissance in England went some way to meet the Church, while the Church, long since disillusioned by the arbitrary edicts and portentous delays of the Vatican, gave a shy but real welcome to the Renaissance. Thus the Renaissance was made respectable and the Church, soon to be the Church of England, was immeasurably enriched.

Nor was knowledge to be wasted on the empty air. For however historians may dispute the relative importance of the cultures and principles which, in conflict on the continent, were to a great extent reconciled in England, one thing is beyond dispute: Henry VIII, by ridding the universities of priests, had made room there for the new ideas and for new men to relish them. The cloisters were cleared and the doors thrown open to let in the day; and among those who passed in at the gate were the sons of England's gentlemen.

When, therefore, the first James came to the throne, the auguries were fair. The new knowledge had the blessing of a reborn and purified Church—a Church which had protested, in the name of national dignity and sheer common sense, and had emerged triumphant in its protest. It was independent and it was enlightened. Joined with the forces of reason and good will, it was to lend heart to Englishmen throughout the most vital enterprise of their history —the subjection of the monarch to the just demands of liberty and conscience. It is certainly true that the processes of honorable dissent had as much to do with the English Revolution as did the established Church; but in the end it was the Church which embodied the middle way, the way of sanity and moderation, and which struck the decisive balance when the House of Stuart, to which, in its alternating arrogance and amiability, the new doctrines had always been alien, came to its final discredit and exile.

When the smoke cleared and the shouting died, a thoughtful Englishman could see that he was left with four clear rules. The spirit behind these rules had long been abroad, had informed the Parliaments and market places, the Sabbath congregations and the Councils of War during a whole century of struggle; but now this spirit, in its hour of victory, could pause awhile so that men might more exactly formulate its teaching. What they had fought for and what they had won might now be made finally plain; the charter of seventeenth-century England might be drawn. Four clear rules, I have said; and they were these:

In the first place, England was never again to tolerate outside interference in any matter of religion or domestic policy. If a man must be a Roman Catholic, then let him look to it that he was an Englishman first. He might be suffered to revere the Pope as the head of his church—though even this was displeasing to sound Protestants; but if once the Pope tried to influence him to a course of political action inside the realm of England, then he obeyed at peril of his head. As for the King and his Ministers, if they wanted to have truck with their grand connections over the Channel, they might cross the Channel and join them, for there was no place for them here.

Secondly, and with particular regard to His Majesty, the King should know that he might tax his people only if he listened to them and respected what he heard. Theoretically, he might still retain a few absolute prerogatives; let him confine himself to exercising that of mercy—and without straining it too hard in favor of his friends. The King ruled not by divine right but by consent of Parliament and people. They had banished one King and beheaded another, and although they disliked such affairs, and were eager to be respectful of His Majesty's person and loyal to his crown, he was to reflect that that crown would not be enlarged to fit a swelling head.

Thirdly, Parliament made laws to restrain the wicked and to ensure the liberty of the righteous. Such laws, enforced impartially and in the light of custom and sound sense, were binding on every man. No one was above the law's reach and no one below its protection. Let judge and jury look to it, and the name of Jeffreys be left to stink as high as his Royal Master's.

Lastly, every man would one day stand accountable for his actions before God. To guide him in these actions God had given him a conscience. Let him then see into that conscience before acting and, having seen, bear himself in accordance with what he saw; and then let friends, neighbors or enemies, kings, captains or prelates, say and do what they might.

The ethic thus portrayed, with its insistence on justice and individual responsibility, may be seen as that of middling people who, having education and energy, despised the prerogatives of those above them and respected the weakness of those below. It was the ethic of an already emerging middle class—at once of the shopkeeper and the small squire; and it was thus the ethic of many born gentle and many more who were rapidly attaining to gentility. In essence dynamic—an ethic of "protestant" achievement—it was yet deeply conservative. For it provided a very solid framework for the nation's affairs; and again, it was so concerned to protect its institutions against illegitimate interference that it effectively protected both those institutions and many less desirable from the proper adjustment that later conditions might dictate. But then the Englishman—and particularly the English gentleman, whose very sense of duty renders him less flexible—has always been prone to erect false constants; what is once right is right forever—roast beef will do as well at Midsummer as at Michaelmas.

5

THE WITHDRAWING ROOM

THE VIRTUES OF THE EIGHTEENTH CENTURY are at present unfashionable, and none less fashionable, than certain prescribed modes of intercourse and address which, giving an elegance of form and texture to the cruder styles of the past, were made the basis of good manners. Let us consider, in this connection, the exigent authority of Lord Chesterfield.

Chesterfield is best known for his letters to his illegitimate son, Philip Stanhope. On their account he has come in for much abuse, it being averred that his values were superficial and arid, his attitudes condescending, his tone peremptory. Eminent critics have asked us to pity the amiable and clumsy Stanhope, representing him as the target of ever more unfeeling demands quite unsuited to his personality or abilities. Only in the grave, as Strachey re-marks, could Stanhope look for respite, and who knew but that even there a letter from his Lordship would follow one explaining how best to comport oneself in that situation . . .? I feel bound to say that there is a good deal in this criticism. The sheer number of Chesterfield's letters is forbidding, and scarce one of them but contained some exercise for the infant Stanhope to complete, or some severe injunction as to what the pubescent Stanhope must do when he came to such a place, or a curt request for an explanation of some social error the mature Stanhope had committed. In these letters we may find concern, affection and even love; but all gave place to Chesterfield's desire to *instruct,* to mold the gawky and unambitious Stanhope into his own ideal of accomplishment and grace.

And yet we should all do well to pay attention to Chesterfield. Leave aside his dignity and assurance—it was Cyril Connolly, I think, who remarked that Chesterfield dismissed death with a few cool and well-bred words, whereas Johnson used to sweat with fear at the mention of it—leave aside his wide intellectual appreciation and the easy exactness of his style, there remains behind his advice a very important principle. This I can make tolerably clear by taking points from just two letters. In letter XCIV Chesterfield remarks that his son may be surprised, during his travels, by the absurd superstitions of Papists, but goes on to point out that people only hold such primitive views because they are either very ignorant or very stupid; it therefore behooves Stanhope to pity them and in no case openly to ridicule or despise them. Again, in letter CXXIV, Chesterfield deposes that Stanhope will meet many people whose intellects are inferior to his own—but this is not to say Stanhope may preen himself; on the contrary, it is his social duty to disguise his superiority, on no account letting his less talented acquaintance feel outclassed or underprivileged. Two unambiguous lessons; and from what these lessons have in common we may easily deduce Chesterfield's central principle of good manners.

For in the end, whether Chesterfield is merely telling Stanhope to clean his teeth regularly or, on a rather higher level, is lauding the virtue of social tolerance, he is saying throughout these letters that Stanhope must *put himself out* in order that other people may feel at ease. It is a question not of equality or social conscience but of what Chesterfield variously calls "civility," "good breeding" or indeed by the term "manners" itself. There is no presumption of a bargee or "an ignorant fellow" being as good a man as Stanhope, who is the educated son, illegitimate or not, of an English peer; it is simply that "civility" or "manners"—not to mention self-interest—require one to please one's fellows, however humble or disagreeable, and not to alienate them. In short, Chesterfield, having had many years' experience of the harsh and grinding mechanics of human society, had decided that the only thing to do was to pour on plenty of oil. So don't laugh at the ridiculous Catholics, my son: You might stir up trouble. And by all means let some blabber-mouthed lout think he is as good a scholar as you are: You will thus retain his good will without forfeiting an iota of your own superiority. Good sense dictates such expedients, while good manners (much the same thing, my dear boy) can easily implement them.

In such urbane admonishment we may find the germ of that celebrated eighteenth-century quality—skepticism. Now, it is commonly assumed that this skepticism was an intellectual thing, that men who prized reason and logic and the classical virtue of moderation would naturally find themselves *intellectually* suspicious of enthusiasms and superstitions. There is clearly a lot in this. The exquisite clarity of Hume or the carefully modulated contempt of Gibbon are certainly the products of reasoned argument. But they are also the products of a style or manner of life; so that I do not think it merely fanciful to connect much of eighteenth-century skepticism not only with rational processes but with the conception of good manners which we have been discussing. One must put oneself out so that others may be at ease. Very well, then: Clearly one must avoid generating too much heat or noise about controversial subjects—one must treat them in a well-bred and *skeptical* fashion, eschewing rant and credulity for one's own part and deploring them in others. At the present day, discussion of religion and politics is discouraged in Officers' Messes as being liable to cause quarrel or offense. Plainly such an embargo would have been intolerable to the civilized and speculative gentlemen of eighteenth-century society; but they were shrewd enough to recognize the dangers and to see that a skeptical tone of address would lessen them. Thus, although their wicked shafts of irony sometimes violated their code of manners by causing mental pain, at least dignity and physical comfort were not imperiled; no one thumped the table, shouted or threw chamber pots. There was control and self-discipline—there was skepticism; and so Lord Chesterfield's canons of conduct were upheld.

A very fair instance of such eighteenth-century procedure is Chesterfield's own easy dismissal of death, to which I referred earlier in this chapter. While this performance was no doubt partly inspired by the reasoned conviction that death, being the end of all, could hold no terrors (or at least by the gnomic appraisal that there was in any case nothing to be done about it), it can almost equally well be seen as an example of simple good manners of a truly Chesterfieldian kind, springing from a polite wish to reassure the company about a disagreeable topic. And here, unfortunately, is the rub. For it is just this kind of behavior which has got the eighteenth century, and Chesterfield in particular, a bad name. In so far as their irony stemmed from social dexterity rather than from intellectual process, Chesterfield and his contemporaries are stigmatized as frivolous and shallow. Their elegance and courage are not allowed to excuse their insincerity, and they are as much distrusted by earnest atheists as they are by earnest Christians.

All of which brings us to a final and most important point. As I have interpreted it here, eighteenth-century skepticism was contemptuous not so much of religion itself as of *intemperate zeal for religion,* this latter being seen as a social nuisance. (Hence the hostility, to Gibbon for example, of our contemporaries who are genuinely *committed,* no matter on which side.) Now, since it was the traditional duty of a gentleman to uphold his country's Church, and since he might well find the duty either ridiculous or irksome, "skepticism" provided him with an invaluable means of compromise—a means readily sanctioned in the sacred name of good manners. For "skepticism," as one form of "breeding," enabled the whole tedious question to be smoothly put aside save for certain brief and ritual observances; and the gentleman was thus allowed—indeed obliged—virtually to ignore his religion without in any way appearing guilty of disloyalty to his Church.

6

RUGBY CHAPEL

"ON ONE OF ITS SIDES," writes G. M. Young in *Portrait of an Age,* "Victorian history is the story of the English mind employing the energy imparted by evangelical conviction to rid itself of the restraints which evangelicalism had laid on the senses and the intellect; on amusement, enjoyment, art; on curiosity, on criticism, on science." This encouraging dictum is well enough; but the writer himself qualifies it, and it would be less than wise to forget those many who, far from opposing evangelical restraint, gloried in it and lived to see their sons and their sons' sons do likewise. For the enlightened, for the rebel, for men of good will and flexible intelligence, Young speaks truly; but for every Edmund Gosse who grew to defy his father's faith, how many more must have knuckled under, at best merely mute and at worst uncomprehending, and stayed down on their knees? And for all Young's optimism, a formidable legacy of restraint remains with us even now. Things may seem very well to those of us who frequent senior common rooms and seldom talk save with men of educated and inquiring minds; but there are dark corners—whole dark areas—of blind ignorance and superstition over much of England to this very day. No doubt George Eliot gave God His *congé* in the gardens of Trinity College;

no doubt Darwin, Huxley and Russell have pronounced and many voices echoed them along the Cam. Even so, not a week before I wrote these lines, a young master in a prominent Kentish preparatory school was roundly rebuked for suggesting to his class, in the most tentative fashion, that perhaps not all of Genesis was absolutely and literally true.

An isolated instance? One may well hope so. But it occurred in the reputable, middle-class surroundings—"educated" surroundings—of a well-found and, of its kind, influential institution. It is enough to remind us that the residual legacy of restraint "on curiosity, on criticism, on science" is not easily set aside, and to send us back to the section of Young's text in which, just before the message of hope which I have quoted above, he writes: "Evangelicalism had imposed on society, even on classes which were indifferent to its religious basis and unaffected by its economic appeal, its code of Sabbath observance, responsibility, and philanthropy; of discipline in the home, regularity in affairs; it had created a most effective technique of agitation, of private persuasion and social persecution." Doubtless, as Young then says, much of the energy and earnestness which lay behind this code was later turned to oppose or at least to moderate it; yet enough of the original doctrine endured—and still endures—for it to be worth examination here.

Broadly surveyed, the case appears thus. Up to about 1840, despite the increasing popular enthusiasm in moral and spiritual affairs, a man was respectable provided he was seen outwardly to conform with the articles and tenets of the Church of England. He might believe in God or he might not—let him only pay decorous lip service to religion, or at least not scoff at it in public, and nothing more was required of him. He might keep a mistress, provided he refrained from flaunting her and continued properly courteous to his wife; he might gamble heavily; he might drink himself under the table; he might associate freely with pugilists and pimps. Religion was not allowed to interfere with private life, and there was an end of it. By the middle of the century, however, religion had overflowed the discreet channels in which it had been hitherto contained and had swamped the whole countryside; it had invaded everything—private life most of all. Superficial conformity, tempered by good taste and good sense, was no longer enough; a man must *believe* and behave as if he believed. The spirit of the evangel, militant and inquisitorial, knowing nothing of fear or favor, searched to the very soul and was the scourge of compromise. His mistress must go or a man must be damned—in this world as well as the next. The parson might hunt no longer and could say farewell to his comfortable rubber at whist. For the Lord God was a jealous God, and from now on He was to be taken seriously. The tinker and the hedge priest had gone forth mouthing out their message and they had found many listeners. Credulity and ignorance had prevailed, and the credulous and the ignorant would allow no quarter—to their betters least of all.

For there was to be no "opting out" for the enlightened, no license or privilege for the great. A man was weighed at the worth of his soul. Acres could not raise this soul, wit and learning could not give it grace—were indeed vanities yet more subtle and misleading than the all too obvious snares of worldly rank or fleshly lust. There was no place now for the easy skepticism, the well-mannered indifference of the previous century, since of all the devil's weapons these were perhaps the most insidious—better that a man sin in hot blood and repent in agony than shrug off evil with a tolerant phrase. The days of "civility" were done—to put a man at his ease was only to smooth his descent to Hell. Salvation was in Christ, so believe on Him and be saved, and suit your words to your belief, not to the dictates of an empty courtesy, a shallow desire to please. Nor is this all: Not only must you preach right, but your actions must follow your preachment, so that in the purity of your life Christ may see the final proof of your belief. The fields and villages had long since heard the solemn injunction; the small towns had heard and then the larger; and finally even London heard—heard and heeded with the rest. For it was the message of the time, a message to which no man might close his ears and live; and to no section of the community was it so sternly imparted, on no class of men was it so firmly enjoined, as on the gentlemen of England.

True, a gentleman's soul was worth no more than a tanner's. But the gentleman was in the public eye; however unjustly, he had "advantages," he *counted;* so let him set the example—or be dragged down from his seat if he failed. Furthermore, the gentleman had a useful office to fulfill, nay more, a sacred trust: As a man of influence and education, he must protect his religion against its enemies. For enemies it had, despite the new-found fervor; nor was there lacking a man of perception and high resolve to find these enemies out. Sitting in his study on the Rugby flats, Dr. Thomas Arnold could see them where they lurked. Lurked? They were strutting boldly forth, equipped with engine and battering ram, heartened by deep and clever counsel, most eager to scale the ramparts of the faithful or tunnel beneath them till they collapsed into the dust. There were two enemies, one from the south and one from the north. The enemy from the south had already enjoyed ample triumphs; he had sent his spies into Oxford, seduced many of her beloved sons—and brought Newman himself over to the old whoremaster of Rome. The proud and passionate man sitting in the study at Rugby knew what that meant: It meant the end of reason, justice and progress, the denial of intellect and the betrayal of freedom. Oh, yes; Dr. Arnold knew what the enemy from the south was after—to make a captive plaything of the soul.

But the enemy from the north was even more vile and, in addition, very much more likely to achieve total success. For in the name of intellect and freedom—the very things the Doctor prized so highly —the enemy from the north desired, not indeed to enslave the soul (in which case at least faith of *some* sort would survive), but to destroy it. Or, more accurately, to deny its existence. The infidel hosts were on the march. Atheists. Nor was theirs the mere frivolous hostility to Christ that was bred of skepticism or indifference; it was a massive, relentless, reasoned and scientific refutation, a refutation as earnest and as formidable as the religion which it sought to discredit. Indeed, it had its roots in the same rich soil as that religion, soil from which it drew the same nourishment—sincerity, courage, integrity and zeal. Had not the Doctor himself approved the first signs of its awakening? The application of reason, the freedom of inquiry . . . ? And now look where it had all led. To the denial of

God, to the denial of Christ as His Son; to the spurning of faith and to the derision of the Church that kept it.

What was to be done? How was he to keep inviolate his fenland fortress—to scotch the venomous thing that had crawled out from under the stones of decaying Rome, and at the same time to oppose the steady and well-routed march of the reasoners? Should he take intellect as his weapon? But then intellect had caused enough trouble already. And besides, it was in short supply. He had a fair share of mature wisdom himself, but his boys were not, by definition, mature, and they were often painfully lacking in mental endowment as well. No; intellect was valuable but unreliable; it could be used, certainly, but in the last resort it must be (however reluctantly) abandoned; and in its place he would set "character." The ramparts of the citadel that was Rugby School would be manned by Christian Gentlemen, adequately primed with carefully chosen knowledge but, above all, armed with the pure faith, the dutiful energy, the persistence for good and detestation of evil, the readiness to interfere and the resistance to taint, all of which the noble term "character" comprehended. And having defended his (and their) ground at Rugby, they should then go out into the world taking his (and now their) gospel of character with them to the great future discomfiture of his (and of course their) enemies of whatever kind and capacity.

But the good Doctor was far too shrewd to overrate the quality of his material. Having already conceded that his boys might be deficient in intellect, he further allowed that they were, in the nature of things, deficient in the moral virtues as well. Vile and libidinous, puffed out with the Old Adam, they must first be shriven before character, in any positive sense, could be induced. The process of shriving was essentially a practical matter. Arnold, taking the introverted evangelical insistence on the state of the soul and, as it were, turning it outward to the world, simply made it plain that wantonness, sloth, treachery, lust and deceit, being displeasing to God and also *dangerous to society*, would be punished by society (to the gratification of God) with outlawry and shame. In this case, of course, Rugby was society and he himself its agent of vengeance;

and no boy came to be fifteen or sixteen without having learned the lesson thoroughly. If he had behaved himself, he was treated with a lofty and generalized approbation. If not, if he had let the Old Adam show in him and thus offended Arnold and society (not to mention God), then he would in any case be vigorously punished, very probably flogged, and even (in cases by no means extreme) expelled. Worst of all, perhaps, he would be made aware of the Doctor's supreme contempt. Thus was the first stage of Arnold's training accomplished; ordeal by fire had amply demonstrated to the boys that vice did not pay; now to persuade them that virtue would.

And so to the positive inducement of character. Arnold would begin by pointing out to his pupils that they were the sons of gentlemen and that it was therefore their business to rule. In the first place, then, let them reflect on what was to be learned from history —history Greek, Roman, and, most of all, Biblical, for the latter was surely richest in the revelation of God. The lesson they had to learn from history was not difficult: They must learn that rulers needed a faith and that the best kind of faith was religious faith, others being less apt to endure. Where there was no faith, or where it was of an inferior (e.g. political) brand, there could only be decline and failure (Imperial Rome and Athens); where true faith was, or had lapsed but been renewed, there would come regeneration and rejoicing (the Israelites). In their own day, what was required of the pupils of Rugby was a renewal of faith, this commodity having been conspicuously rare during the last hundred and fifty years and the lamentable consequences plain for all to see.

The next stage in instruction brought a certain refinement. Arnold, being mistrustful of evangelical introversion and of obsession with the soul, would make two controversial propositions—controversial, that is, for his own time. He would insist that his pupils should use their faith to attend to their country's affairs, both high and low; and he would further insist that they must interpret their faith in the light of recent developments in science and scholarship. For while Arnold held rational infidelity in abhorrence, he remained a man of reason and saw clearly that if religious belief, on the one hand, and scientific and textual criticism, on the other, were not somehow reconciled, then science, ultimately, would come off the victor. If to us this conception seems anything but original, I should remark that in the educational circles of Arnold's day it was a resounding heresy and gave rise to the most bitter and damaging complaint against him.

At this stage the intellectual part of Arnold's instruction ceased. Penetrating it might be, but, as we have seen, intellectual doctrine was to play only a subsidiary role, and by now there had been enough of it. (I need hardly point out that most of the more frivolous or joyous portions of classical literature—Aristophanes, the Greek lyrics, the Odes of Horace or the shrewd advice of Ovid— were dealt with largely by omission.) Intellect, used to display the historical theory of character, had fulfilled its function; it was now time for character itself to be imparted. Faith, and the political usages of faith, had been explained; now let the doctrine come to practice. Let the boys begin to rule by ruling other boys. And rule they did, with the distant but all-seeing eye of Arnold upon them and with the dire, obsessive knowledge that to break trust would be to court instant damnation both by Arnold and by God.

Such a system, enforced by sanctions at once so plausible and so terrible, could make or break a boy for life. (It made Stanley and it broke Clough.) Small wonder that Arnold's prefects, the products of what we might call his extroverted and systematized evangelicalism, were the subjects of respectful remark wherever they went. Primed with faith, assured of the excellence of their code and the supreme beneficence of their intentions, intellectually fortified by the Doctor's wary interpretation of history and politics, they were the unbreakable Life Guard of the new respectability. For the shock troops of evangelicalism had done their work; now was the time for consolidation, and this must be the task of a body more educated and more disciplined than the early enthusiasts, a body less hysterical and individual, a body that could combine long and expert training with a broad and humane sense of mission and, let it never be forgotten, was additionally blessed with the manners and bearing of gentlemen. In the person of Arnold, gentility had taken over evangelicalism; it had acknowledged its timeliness, quietly disposed of its extravagances, given it a stiffening of intellect and the deep polish of good breeding, and had then set it up, recognizable but transformed, as the central pillar of society. Meanwhile, the Life Guard of Dr. Arnold's pupils, later to be strengthened by thousands of the pupils of his imitators and successors, had formed about the pillar to present a massive defense in depth. Cry God for Arnold, and who would be so bold as to ride against his Regiment? There could be no doubt: Responsibility, philanthropy, "regularity in affairs"; faith, duty, sobriety; chastity and prudence; "private persuasion and social persecution"—all these must henceforth be strictly accounted in any reckoning of the English gentleman, because he was now, without possibility of escape, a "Christian" gentleman as well.

7

SYNTHESIS

EACH OF THE SIX previous chapters has treated of one element in what I regard as the English tradition of gentility. The treatments have all been brief, not to say oversimplified; but in each case I have, I hope, made the central point tolerably plain.

I now propose to combine the six elements I have described into a synthesis. By this means I hope to reconstruct the tradition of English gentility as it might have been stated in approximately 1900— the final period, that is to say, during which the gentleman's prestige was still unimpaired, his ethical and social relevance still unquestioned. From 1900 onward the fortunes and standards of the gentleman were both to decline—more latterly, indeed, to disintegrate; and it is therefore doubly important that we should catch the spirit of the tradition at this particular time, since hitherto all its developments had been definite enrichments, whereas all subsequent changes, being expedient shifts and betrayals made in response to hostile pressures, were only to be for the worse. In 1900, then, we shall catch the gentleman at his high point; we shall see him, albeit for the last time, in a pure state, and we shall thus be in a proper position to discuss his degeneration, in that we shall know who and what he was before he started to degenerate. In making my synthesis I shall not, of course, find all the six elements I have discussed as being of equal importance; and it is also clear that separate elements may be seemingly at sharp odds with one another—eighteenth-century skepticism, for example, being an awkward bedfellow for Arnoldian dedication. But when this happens, we shall find help in the English capacity for compromise; nor is it, in principle, difficult to conceive that a gentleman of 1900, assisted by good sense and the passage of time, might have been well able to modify his grandfather's religious zeal with a touch of recaptured eighteenth-century elegance. In any event, let us deal with such contradictions as we come to them and pass without further delay to sum up the tradition of gentility as it was in the last days of the gentleman's pre-eminence.

It would be untrue to say that the English gentleman, as such, was ever much infected with the Greek passion for intellectual inquiry. On the other hand, the Greek concern for reason and truth have always regulated the gentleman's conduct of practical affairs. Set an administrative or legal problem before him, and he will be scrupulous both in his pursuit of the facts and in his efforts to establish their logical interdependence. Facing facts, keeping cool and playing fair: These virtues, surely descended from the sweet reasonableness of the Greeks, have continued to pay high dividends in efficiency and justice. They are, too, entirely compatible with freedom; for while the tyrant must make *a priori* judgments, disregarding the logical or human state of the case and seeing only his own obsessional purpose, the free man is free, above all, to search out the truth, to speak and act on his findings.

But if the gentleman is free to serve the truth, he is not free to serve himself. The Greeks saw, of course, that even a gentleman must have the use of money; but they forbade him to grovel for it. If he was reduced to earning his living, that was his misfortune and he was to be pitied; even so he must not sell himself sexually or politically, engage in the meaner forms (*i.e.* practically any form) of commerce, and on no account must he work with his hands—save only to fight with them for his city. Basically, the rule was that no free citizen might engage himself to any enterprise in order to make a monetary profit; once his living was secured, he must occupy himself in a manner worthy of a free man—in exercise, conversation and the good government of his city and his own dependents.

Now, the English gentleman has always been more flexible in his choice of occupation than his continental counterpart. Even so, he has held, more or less, to the old Greek rule. Except in an emergency (or for a hobby) he still does not work with his hands (it is significant that under the Geneva Convention no prisoner of commissioned rank may be put to physical labor); and insofar as he has joined in commerce, he has either tended to admit loss of caste (however ironically) or else has persuaded himself that he is in fact acting for the general good rather than his own individual profit. I shall be told, I know, that there have been famous "aristocratic" banking houses, that Etonians do brisk business in Lloyd's and on the floor of the Exchange; but even today such people insist that their "real" life is elsewhere—on their country estates or in their libraries—and in 1900, which is the operative date for this discussion, their numbers were far less and their protests yet more elaborate. Even in 1900 it would of course have been absurd to say that *no one* could go into business and remain a gentleman; but we may just take note that "business" men of the better type have always been suspiciously ready to apologize for their own activities and quite neurotically zealous to deplore those of their colleagues. In the last resort, then, a gentleman whose money comes from "business" does his damnedest to pretend it comes from something—from almost anything—else.

But the English, lacking the delicacy and quickness of the Greeks,

have always had more in common with the Romans. *Pietas,* loyalty
to family, to country, to local and national institutions and gods, has
come as second nature to the Englishman; while *gravitas* and *dignitas,* in their unwieldy way, have done more to form his character
than any amount of Greek seemliness.

But fortunately or otherwise, *gravitas* implied the same course
of conduct as that advocated by the Greeks, albeit for very different
reasons: *Gravitas* meant that freeborn gentlemen must avoid mean
employment, *not* so that they might be free (as the Greeks would
have had them) for cultural intercourse, but because mean or
monetary occupations detracted, in the most open manner, from
the social and moral weight which any gentleman or political ruler
must possess. *Dignitas* was also, of course, involved, as was downright snobbery—snobbery, because we are now coming up against
the merely static process of keeping up appearances as opposed to
the dynamic (Greek) process of developing the personality. But
let the subtleties be what they may, the main point was taken: *Gravitas, i.e.* a suitable and weighty attitude, and *dignitas,* the outward
appearance to match it, were categorically required of any gentleman, who was not, therefore, free to take up common or debasing
pursuits.

But it would be unfair to conclude that the Roman influence
made only for social prohibitions and the self-conscious display of
aloofness. There was, though hardly in the creative Greek sense, a
positive side to it all. The display of hauteur was not just for the
sake of display, it was to give prominence and authority to the gentleman as the living embodiment of *pietas.* For it was his duty to
enforce on others the demands which *pietas* made of himself—a
duty which the English gentleman has always accepted with as
much conviction as his Roman predecessor. Loyalty to country, to
family, to the gods (or God); a man who is charged with such
obligations, and is charged, moreover, with seeing they are fulfilled
by others, must necessarily be allowed to pass his days unembar-
rassed by trivial or menial demands on his time and energy. He is
the guardian of higher things; and as such he is unquestionably
entitled to certain services of the body and certain privileges of

dress, maintenance and general estate, so that his guardianship may be worthily upheld.

Whatever dispute there may be about occupations suitable for a gentleman, one has always been considered suitable—fighting. A man with a taste for battle could always aspire to rise in the social scale, while any gentleman of reckonable standing has always owed a duty to his superiors to fight at their call, to his underlings to fight for their protection. I went into this matter at some length in my chapter on feudalism, and I do not wish to repeat myself here; but three points will, I think, bear re-emphasis. First, the traditional reward for military service is land; and although successful soldiers are no longer enfeoffed, even today few things are reckoned more becoming to a gentleman, when he is not under arms or giving other service to his country, than the supervision of his estates. Secondly, we should remember that although the term "gentleman," in its broad sense, denotes an amalgam of many and diverse qualities, in its narrow sense it is actually a rank in the social hierarchy: A man of family or parts, who did not qualify by his accouterment or following for knighthood and was not employed in honorable attendance as an esquire, was accorded the lowest of the "petty noble" or gentle ranks—was called, that is, a gentleman. To be a gentleman in the broader sense, it is necessary to possess this minimal qualification of rank; but it is a qualification, in England at least, which has always been readily attained by those who deserved it, for though it may be conferred by birth it can also be conferred by service or by merit. Gentility, then, so far from being a strictly aristocratic preserve, is clearly seen to extend well down into what was, even in feudal times, a potential middle class. Thirdly, there is something to be said of "honor": Let us pass over, for the time being, the more ridiculous embellishments of the code and simply note here that the basis of true honor was the ready fulfillment of mutual obligation or sworn contract. "I am your liege man of life and limb"; the oath was broken often enough, God knows, but for those who took it seriously it constituted an abiding dictate of honorable practice. To speak broadly, the oath was more solemnly treated in England than elsewhere; and almost to this very day English gentlemen have been famous throughout the world for holding to their spoken word.

To integrity they have joined independence. Not only have they held by their word, but they have been shy neither of what they said nor to whom they said it. For by the end of the seventeenth century the fight had been won. There would be no interference from outside with English affairs or persons—whether by the Pope in Rome or by his anointed Emperor—and there would be precious little tolerated, what was more, even from the lawfully crowned King. The King was the titular head of the state and still commanded the allegiance, the oath and the love of Englishmen; but he must respect the laws and institutions which they had set up to safeguard their rights as free and God-fearing citizens. And as to fearing God, they would fear Him in their own time and their own way, holding their own good consciences answerable. There was to be no dictation here—a point of which the King, and for that matter God Himself, had better take good notice.

But though often rugged in address and fierce for his personal rights, the Englishman was always far too sensible to make trouble when it could be avoided. He was a lover of peace and good humor; and thus, though he might suspect the more exaggerated styles which, by the middle of the eighteenth century, were beginning to adorn social intercourse, it was clear to him that a certain elegance would not come amiss. For by such means good order, always dear to his heart, could be preserved, dangerous moments bridged over, acts of rebellion or bad taste promptly and quietly quelled. All that was necessary was to put oneself out a little in order to accommodate others. If a man was a fool, then to tell him so would not mend his folly; find another fool and let them match each other. If one could give pleasure by telling a harmless lie, tell it; the Devil would stay in Hell, and if God had any objections, it was time He looked to His Own manners. Let us have good sense, ease of bearing, well-phrased and relevant talk; and let us not spoil our own pleasure or other people's by getting ill-tempered over some matter just because we happen to think it important. If it is important (a doubtful condition in any case whatever) then it will be none the worse for light handling, which will suit those who are skeptical and allow those who are not to keep their own reservations. Certain aspects of religion must be attended to so that the poor and ignorant may have a proper example and keep their proper place; but a man may hear a Sunday sermon in a well-warmed pew without sniveling and driveling about the state of his soul for the other six days of the week.

Unfortunately, however, those who had no possessions other than their souls were determined that the matter be more seriously regarded—by their social superiors as well as by themselves. It is not my business here to speculate on the origins of evangelical fervor (though one might hazard that it had its birth, along with most superstitious movements, in popular discontent). It is enough to remark that such fervor existed and spread, and that by 1840 nobody, even if he were proof against religious enthusiasm for his own part, could be proof against the clamorous and sickening attitudes which such enthusiasm inspired in others. Whether he would or no, the gentleman must join in the hymn singing and admit that salvation was not to be had without amendment of life. He must believe; and if he must believe, then he must believe every day of the week (not just in his well-warmed pew on Sunday) and suit his daily actions to his belief. In a word, he must be moral; not merely kind or thoughtful or well mannered, but *pure;* and this meant getting rid of his concubine as well as being considerate to his wife.

A lot to ask? Unnecessary? Of course. The whole thing was tiresome in the extreme. And yet it must be at once acknowledged that it was a tremendous source of strength. For the gentleman, having put himself forth with great determination in the seventeenth century and having won the day for freedom and conscience, had tended to rest on his laurels during the ensuing hundred years. He was becoming positively frivolous. While that might be all very well in men who were content merely to be of good birth and take the spoils, it would not do for a class whose very existence depended on service and obligation. Not that the gentleman had ceased, during the eighteenth century, to serve and to oblige; but he was beginning to do so more as a matter of good humor or even of vanity than as a duty and a trust. It was time for a little moral pressure, and if evangelicalism administered something of an overdose, then the gentleman, after all, was well able to take care of himself. As indeed he did. He appointed Dr. Arnold; and the Doctor saw to it that the generations confided to him, while they kept their faith pure, neither neglected such powers of reasoning as they had nor forgot that the proper product of faith was works. His pupils reared their works over the breadth of a growing Empire; and as they reared them they saw, being practical men, that the Doctor's faith might benefit from a little modification—*must* indeed be modified if its works were still to grow. The robust good sense of their great-grandfathers had never been far below the surface. Once more men decided that it was uncalled-for to take up angry or impetuous attitudes over so very delicate, not to say dubious, a topic as God—particularly when there were so many other matters to be dealt with; and once more, even if he were unconscious or disapproving of the recent rationalist victories at the expense of revealed religion, the gentleman decided that, formal observance apart, the affair might be left to settle itself. The compromise was characteristic and tasteful, but the evangelical legacy was still powerful; so that the new decline in religious faith, being both gradual and guilty, did little as yet to impair the sense of practical, secular, and moral obligation which evangelicalism had reawakened.

And so at last we may see and sum our paragon, the English Gentleman in the last days of his ascendancy. We see that he was an agent of justice and effective action, having the fairness and the thoroughness to examine facts and the integrity to act on his findings. We see that he had much regard for the old loyalties—to country, to kinsmen, to Church—and that as a guardian of such institutions, and no less to assist him in his other duties, he saw fit to adopt a grave and somewhat aloof attitude of mind which was matched by dignified demeanor and a superior, though not an ostentatious, style of maintenance. Deeply conservative, if only as a result of fostering the loyalties with which he was charged, he never forgot

his status as a warrior, was always ready, in time of need, to return
to the ancient proving ground of his kind; but when there was no
call for service, then he preferred to remain on the lands which his
ancestors had won by service, for on these lands were at once his
proper establishment and his proper occupation. Lacking the passion for intellectual exchange which had made city life tolerable
for the Greeks, he held firmly to the Greek rule which pronounced
most urban employments to be degrading. He went to the city,
therefore, only to carry out his duties as a ruler—for to rule and to
administer were among the many obligations on which his honor
was based. According to this notion of honor, he was bound not
only by such commonplace rules of decency as chivalry to women
and charity to the poor but by a direct and imperative necessity to
pay for his privileges by rendering service—service to his Sovereign
and his superiors in office, service to his dependents, service to his
Church. But even so he set store by his freedom; if he met his
obligations it was because honor bade him do so, not because any
absolute authority compelled him. Authority he certainly recognized, but only such as his conscience suffered him to obey; he
would welcome laws made by man in proper form and would ac-
knowledge a King who ruled with his consent and with regard for
his interests; but he would brook nothing from a tyrant who claimed
divine right or a priest who dictated through dogma, and in no case
whatever would he accept interference from beyond the sea. As his
position required, he had pleasing manners intended to reassure his
inferiors and to show the proper respect, free of any hint of servility,
to those above him; and he was liable to combine such manners
with a light skepticism which eschewed enthusiasms and quarrels.
But if ever he was tempted to let this skepticism affect his deeper
attitudes, then he was apt to receive timely reminder that many of
his countrymen took their souls—and his—very seriously, and that
if he was to continue in his place, then he must look to his morals.
For the English gentleman, over and above all, was the product of
English morality—a morality compatible with all forms of social and
practical endeavor, but none the less grounded, as deep and firm as

the roots of the oak tree were grounded in English soil, in the stubborn prohibitions of St. Paul.

It is now time to transpose our rather shadowy conception into more concrete terms, so that we may see our man in the round, with all his strength and all his faults, before we go on to consider, in Part Two, the evil fate that will overtake him. Born in 1875, let us say, Matthew James Tench was the eldest child of the rector of a Somerset parish (who had been given the living by his wife's unpretentiously noble second cousin). Until the age of twelve he was educated at home, being taught Latin, Greek and the rudiments of mathematics by his father, being given a smattering of French and music by his mother; he was encouraged to follow all country pursuits—his father refrained from hunting but saw his son well mounted—and was allowed to make friends with the sons of landowners and even tenant farmers, but not with the sons of laborers. He attended the services in his father's church punctually and regularly, but Christianity was not much discussed in his home; it was of course assumed without any question at all to be the one true faith and the ultimate basis of conduct, just as it was assumed that the children of the house would be confirmed, as a matter of routine, at the age of ten; but all these assumptions were so effortless that there could be no point in canvassing religion outside church hours—not even in order to broach its merits. The Rector, in fact, was suspected by his colleagues of lack of zeal, and indeed he was an old-fashioned churchman who had regarded the recent and hysterical trends in the religous life of his country with distaste and alarm. He had told Matthew (Biblically named, but not extravagantly so) how a Christian gentleman behaved, and then instructed him to behave like one. Since there was no nagging and the terms of the enjoinment were broad, the treatment was a complete success: Matthew at first behaved as he was told because he had been kindly told, and later continued because he found it a decent, sensible and by no means uncomfortable fashion of behavior.

Packed off to one of the less distinguished Oppidan houses at

Eton, Matthew spent five years learning to make elegant Greek and Latin verses and how to live at peace with his fellows. These required that he should either share their tastes, which tended to be sporting and bloodthirsty, or, if he must have his own, should refrain from boring other people with them. He found, in fact, that eccentricity was pardonable (in this he was very lucky in his school), but that interference and talebearing were not. In any case, he had little wish to be eccentric and none at all to improve others against their will. He learned that a lot of people were much wealthier than his father and belonged to circles altogether more munificent and powerful; he also learned that these circles were open to himself on certain terms, the main burden of which was that he should make himself agreeable. He discovered that some people in these circles took it for granted, like his father in his humbler way, that they had some function to fulfill for the general good, whilst others, who were apparently no less esteemed, were happy to enjoy their blessings and leave matters at that. Being a boy of good presence and sound sense, he contrived to make several friends from among his contemporaries of whatever type; to keep out of trouble, on the whole, but being in, to bear himself with credit; to attain (though he had little mental curiosity) to a tolerable academic place; to become captain of his house at cricket; to form one romantic but never quite sexual attachment; but still to be as far as ever, at the end of five years, from knowing what to do with his life. The eldest son, he could expect a moderate inheritance; but one thing did seem clear to him, even in the tolerant climate of Eton—that it was not becoming his father's son simply to do nothing at all. He was unthinking, insensitive and ignorant; but he knew that a gentleman must, in more senses than one, endeavor to pay his way.

However, decision might be postponed awhile, as he was now to go for four years to Oxford. Here he discovered, as he had always suspected, that his gifts were nothing out of the ordinary and that he was clearly destined, even with his mother's connections and his father's money, to live an unspectacular life. And so, having taken a low honors degree (Third in Mods, Fourth in Greats), and conscious of what was proper to his caste, he went with his parents' blessing into a sound but unspectacular regiment of horse. As an officer, he was known for his good humor in the mess, his fairness to his men, and a conscientious performance, not to be remarked in his more glittering colleagues, of uncongenial tasks; he also won repute as an active leader during the Boer War; but shortly afterwards his father died, and he resigned his commission in order to attend to his inheritance.

By the time his mother had been given a suitable pension, his sisters allowed dowries and his two brothers, one in the Church, the other an aspiring barrister, presented with small annuities, he had some £2,000 a year and a passable bit of capital left for himself. He could also look to inherit from his mother a small estate in Wiltshire, which had come to her from an aunt and on which she proposed to live henceforth. He was, therefore, tolerably well off (and potentially landed) and he had enjoyed an excellent conventional education; grounded in the traditional disciplines, he had, in addition, valuable experience of men—including the lower class—and of some unfamiliar countries. It was plain what he must do: His early background (team spirit, good form, acceptance), his good sense and lack of inconvenient brilliance, his ideas of duty and his easy manner in company, his comfortable provision and his excellent presence, all alike made it suitable—almost, indeed, inevitable—that he should be put to govern his countrymen from their elected Parliament at Westminster. The father of an Etonian friend (who knew an uncle of his mother's) was glad to help, and in 1903, now at the age of twenty-eight and in the prime of life, Captain Matthew James Tench, D.S.O., bowed to the Speaker and took his seat on the Conservative side of the House.

We shall hear more of Matthew Tench as our argument proceeds; we shall see him at times when things will not be so well with him, when the years and what they bring will have rotted his early assurance in the duties, excellence and privilege of his kind. But meanwhile, since he is a representative figure for our purpose, I would draw attention to two points. First, in 1903, when he takes his seat, neither Matthew nor anyone else questions his right to be

a legislator. His political experience is nil, his abilities and aware-
ness limited, but everyone is confident that *his moral character as a
gentleman* will be entirely adequate to see him through this and
even more important tasks. Secondly, and almost more significant,
I would ask you to distinguish Matthew the gentleman from the
mere member of the upper class. For while Matthew has been more
fortunate than many gentlemen's sons (Eton, Oxford, a private income), he is yet of relatively humble origin (the country rectory)
and, most important of all, though he accepts his position as his due,
he realizes that it can only be finally justified by service and by duty.

Take the matter of occupation. Matthew's have been honorable,
even coveted—an Army officer and now a ruler—but he has never
been in doubt that he must *have* an occupation, because he has
been brought up, as the son of a modest Christian gentleman, to
understand that he is under an obligation to make himself of use.
Had he been merely of the upper class, had moral scruple not operated to make him a gentleman as well, he would have been quite
content to enjoy his income at leisure; for whereas the gentleman
always seeks to deserve his position, the aristocrat, disdainful and
insouciant, is quite happy just to exploit it. As it happens, the next
part of this book will open with a discussion of upper-class attitudes,
so I do not propose to linger on them here. But it will be appropriate,
by way of concluding this initial portrait of the gentleman, to emphasize once more the fundamental ethical difference which sets
him apart from the aristocrat. The aristocrat, then, is concerned to
demonstrate his status by consumption, possession and display; the
gentleman, while he knows that his position requires of him dignity
and a solid style of living, sets his store on performance and not on
show. To the aristocrat, badges, trappings, banquets and titles are
the true ends of his pride; to the gentleman such ornaments serve
only to lend seemliness to his office and so to ensure that he will
be the more readily and faithfully assisted in discharging it. The
aristocrat avoids the menial task because he sees it as distasteful, the
gentleman because it is unworthy; the aristocrat spurns business
because he is, as he thinks, above money, the gentleman because,

once he has a mere sufficiency, he is indifferent to it. For if nothing else has been made clear in Part One of this book, I trust that one point at least has gone home: The life of the English gentleman is centered on one purpose—to recognize and to honor his obligation and his trust.

PART TWO

Degeneration

At the head of this class we may justly rank the worship of images . . .

—Gibbon, *Decline and Fall of the Roman Empire*, Ch. xlix.

But the subjects of the Byzantine Empire, who assume and dishonour the names both of Greeks and Romans, present a dead uniformity of abject vices, which are neither softened by the weakness of humanity nor animated by the vigour of memorable crimes.

—Gibbon, *Decline and Fall of the Roman Empire*, Ch. xlviii.

THE AGE OF THE GOSSIP COLUMN

I HAVE ALREADY SAID something of the difference between the notions which govern the conduct and customs of the upper class and those which go to form the ideal of gentility. It is time to come closer to the matter, time that I should render a more precise answer to the question: "What, in any case, do you mean by the upper class?"

I take the upper class to be that section of the British people which, in relation to its very limited number, enjoys by established right the most conspicuous share of the country's amenities and of the people's (not necessarily favorable) regard. This it may do for one or more of several reasons, some of them implying real abilities (of whatever kind), some not. Thus a man may achieve the prestige and standards of consumption which stamp him as upper-class variously through inherited or acquired wealth, through professional, social, athletic or artistic success, through political power (which, like money, may be either inherited or acquired), or, especially if it is combined with wealth or land, through mere social rank. (The only proviso for an "acquired" qualification is that it should also be enduring.) The upper class as at present constituted will therefore include Mr. Gaitskell along with Mr. Macmillan, most serving generals, the Duke of Bedford and Lady Lewisham, Archbishop Fisher (whose prestige and influence, although he has retired, are still reckonable), Noel Coward and Somerset Maugham, Mr. Billy Wallace and Mr. Uffa Fox, Sir Bernard Docker and Mr. Hugh Fraser, Sir Laurence Olivier, Evelyn Waugh, the Provost of King's College, Cambridge, and the Warden of Wadham College, Oxford, Dr. Robert Birley of Eton, and Mr. Antony Armstrong-Jones. Some of these have reached their positions only after exerting great abilities (meritoriously or otherwise), whereas some have been born or simply drifted into them; some are gentlemen and some are not; some have real power and influence, others only a brilliant and perhaps ephemeral cachet; some will lose caste when they lose or retire from office; some despise display and some care for little else. But all have this in common: By virtue of their position, however these have been attained, they are able to call upon an enormous store of the world's benefits as these are commonly conceived. Archbishop Fisher enjoys outstanding professional repute, Mr. Fraser has wealth, Somerset Maugham has both; Dr. Birley rules the most famous school in the world; the generals have hundreds of thousands of men at their beck and personal establishments appropriate to this situation; and Mr. Armstrong-Jones has walked slap into a fairy tale. These people are top people; they are of the upper class because whether they like it or not (and some of them don't) they control or consume the cream of the country's resources—its cash, its offices, its perquisites, its youth—and only have to open their mouths in a yawn to be assured of an attentive and nationwide hearing.

Now as I see it, the really significant thing is that these and all other members of the upper class make their appeal to the popular imagination through, and only through, external appurtenance. However history may rate Mr. Macmillan as a statesman, and however he may rate himself, he is, to the public, the man with £10,000 a year who lives at 10 Downing Street and hobnobs with Khrushchev and Her Majesty the Queen: a top person among top people. Dr. Birley, an honorable man who is deeply conscious that he has a thousand minds to mold and a thousand souls in his keeping, is seen and valued, not as a scholar or an educationalist, but as a photogenic figure in cassock and bands who has the privilege, should he care to exercise it, of birching noble bottoms. Noel Coward is reckoned, not as a brilliantly versatile actor who has himself written a body of witty, perceptive and soundly constructed plays, but as a wealthy *flaneur* in a white dinner jacket who tosses off virulent remarks of questionable moral taste to the pleasure-seeking company in whichever exotic resort he is currently avoiding British rates of income tax. The upper class, in short, is assessed in terms cither of overt monetary status and luxury absorption or at least of directly appreciable privilege. It is not popularly assessed, even where such an assessment would be easily possible, in terms of past achievement or present virtue.

What is worse, the externals used for popular reference and judgment are, even in their own kind, the shoddiest and the cheapest. The standards applied are those of the gossip columnist, who seeks to render comprehensible to gutter mentalities the supposed sophistication and glamour of high society. This is attempted by constant and unctuous use of luxury symbols, such as "caviar" and "champagne"; the quality is seldom specified but there is a note in heavy type as to the amounts consumed. Also receiving the accolade of heavy type are titles, makes of car, names of smart holiday resorts, the computed cost of entertainments and whatever new gimmick is being currently celebrated. *"Lady Jane was giving a Navels Party.* All present had come with some new form of decoration to wear in their navels." Or, "Champagne flowed with a difference in 37 Uckley Mews. It was being drunk from a selection of *Lord Lesley's famous collection of dead actresses' footwear."* If the gathering in question should have any genuine or cultural importance, that particular aspect of it is heavily mocked (*"His Royal Highness* made a wry face at the pictures."); while any person of serious or intellectual distinction is liable to be pilloried on that account ("Mr. Potts surveyed the brilliant scene with the jaundiced look of one who has spent a lifetime in critical studies.") and to the inferred discredit of endeavor or intellect. Myself, I would have less objection to judgment being made from externals if only those externals had one particle of quality or value—such as we might find in fine houses, rare furniture or even in elegant and analytical gossip; but the sugaricing values which at present prevail in all accounts of "upper-class" affairs, the gossip which goes no further than to specify a recent title or to estimate a crookedly earned income, seem to me to touch the final floor of degradation. One might, after all, be just prepared to admire a blood cousin of the Queen, even if his only virtue lay in the cousinhood; but one can hardly be impressed by the adopted daughter of an impotent press baron or the younger son of a marquis who has opened a coffee bar.

But although current standards in all this may be peculiarly vile, we should remember that the upper class has always depended, for its prestige, on external display of some sort or another. And here we come to the most deplorable circumstance of all: The majority of the upper class is not only content to be judged by outsiders after this superficial fashion but itself accepts as valid such means of evaluation. The toys and ribands which impress the vulgar are just as impressive to those who own and wear them; the upper class as a whole, though not quite accepting the debased criteria of William Hickey's column, is nevertheless prone to assess itself solely in terms of material possession and overt privilege. This is not necessarily true of individuals, and it is perhaps least likely to be true of those who have been longest and most firmly established. The overall impression remains that matters such as precedence, personal decoration and awards, style of living, entertainment and travel, publicly recognized sexual success and the right to public obedience are paramount considerations to all save the most dedicated or disinterested members of the upper class.

I do not need to point out how repugnant such a state of affairs must be to those who accept the notions of gentility, together with its obligations and duties, which I have described in Part One of this essay. What must be noted, however, is that this upper-class conception of status (not as the incidental concomitant of office or responsibility but as an end in itself) ceases to be merely immoral and becomes positively dangerous in a society in which communication is swift and wide and in which, moreover, it is posited as a basic tenet of democracy that what is good for one is good for all. For in such a society upper-class attitudes are no longer confined to the court and the castle, they are no longer merely instances of human vanity to be added to the repertoire of poet and jester; they are known about, read about, daily discussed by every plowboy and shopgirl in the land, and so become not only a matter for envy (which they have always been) but also, by democratic right, a matter for emulation. The result of this process will be discussed later. Meanwhile we must tackle another and parallel social phenomenon which is equally inimical to the tradition of gentility: Having dealt with the preference, both popular and aristocratic, for what is spurious, we must now reverse the medal and deal with the corresponding contempt for what is genuine.

2

THE AGE OF RESENTMENT

EXTERNAL DISPLAY, while it doubtless invites envy, also provides the palliative of hope. The fact that motorcars, fur coats or expensive holidays may be won for a few shillings by anyone who knows the address of a bookmaker does much to make acceptable the inequality with which such benefits are normally distributed. The only god who is truly democratic (apart from Death) is Luck, and any day she may turn full face to a man with her favors. Besides which, despite the Puritan who lurks in all Englishmen, most of us take a carnival delight in witnessing rare or sumptuous exhibition; so that Lady Docker's gold-plated Daimler, for example, is received by many with the same good humor and relish as the Queen's coronation coach.

What people do *not* suffer gladly is that certain individuals should possess unusual *personal qualities*—qualities independent of wealth or possessions and which, of their nature, are not to be won in a pool or a crossword competition. For to allow that a man may have such qualities is to admit the possibility of personal excellence and so, inevitably, of personal superiority. And this, of course, will not do at all. With a little bit of luck, any of us might have been sitting in Lady Docker's Daimler or even, by the appropriate accident of birth, in the Queen's coach, and we can therefore cheerfully and plausibly claim that we are "just as good as" Lady Docker or the Queen; but it is not so easy to maintain this fiction of equality in the face, let us say, of superior intelligence or resolution. True, intelligence itself is bestowed, so to say, by antenatal lottery; but a man who hasn't got it can never win it, and in any case it belongs so very intimately to a person that it can never be dismissed, like wealth or titles, as a mere chance of birth which in no way confers superiority on its possessor. Intelligence, then, and indeed any form of ability are apt to incite the resentment of the unprovided; and when we come to qualities such as courage and selflessness, which require a rigid and personal discipline unconnected with any form of chance, then resentment swells beyond all bounds. For such phenomena dispose once and for all of the comfortable fallacy that *"we are as good as them."*

It follows that it is not so much material possessions in themselves which excite mistrust as the privileges, material or prestigial, which accrue from personal merit and, most of all perhaps, the merit from which they accrue. Possessions as such are readily understood and easily withdrawn by legislation; merit is inalienable, an ever present menace to the self-esteem of the mediocre. During the war, a general like Montgomery, who was careful (in public at least) to give credit for every success to his troops and endeavored to discard the privilege associated with his station, was rapturously received; whereas Lord Alexander, who always retained a certain air of aloofness (there is extant a portrait in which, almost symbolically, he appears in riding boots), made little appeal to the public and was actively disliked by some sections of it. Or yet again, the wartime public was curiously indifferent to tales of the anonymous rich gorging themselves in expensive restaurants, but flew into a rage the moment it heard of important officers or politicians receiving preferential treatment. The lesson is plain: You can have anything you can lay your hands on so long as you do not claim merit or the reward of merit, and even privilege may be tolerated provided that it is a privilege *in vacuo,* as it were, and has not been accorded on account of personal achievement or excellence.

Now, one obvious point about the tradition of gentility we have been examining is that it demands personal excellence. Excellence of a limited kind, certainly, but excellence nevertheless. And it is just this which contemporary opinion is least disposed to recognize —is indeed virulently zealous to deny. Even the modest yet dignified style of maintenance which a gentleman assumes is in one sense more of an affront to the populace than the most lavish display of the wealthy, because the former is associated with the privilege that comes from endeavor or merit, while the latter may be only the casual expression of the good fortune which any typist might acquire tomorrow from a two-and-sixpenny permutation. The traditional qualities and rewards of a mere gentleman are therefore not to be endured; and the consequent process of denigration is at once simple and instructive.

To understand this process we have only to consider contemporary reaction to some of the notions which we discussed earlier. Thus we saw that the contribution of the ancient Greeks to the English ideal of gentility lay in a willingness to seek out the truth and to speak and act in accordance with it. But the age we live in is an age of question begging. Truth and logic must give place to the democratic requirement that nobody at all shall be "offended" or "humiliated." Plain speaking and necessary action are therefore at a heavy discount. A man who is sacked for incompetence must always, in current parlance, have been "victimized." A child who is too idle or too stupid to pass an elementary examination is "maladjusted" or "underprivileged"; and more emphasis will be placed on teaching half-wits to work in raffia than on developing the sorely needed gifts of the brilliant—who are, or so one may suppose, "overprivileged" and therefore to be resented if not feared. If the truth is not palatable to any substantial section of the community (no matter how debased, ignorant or superstitious that section may be), then expedience dictates that the truth be suitably adjusted; "the feeling of the country," or some such meaningless phrase, will be used as an excuse for obscuring facts and delaying proper action, and possible resentment will have been put to rest at the price of verity. We need labor the point no further: We have shoved truth to the bottom of her well and slammed the lid on.

Nor have the old loyalties, the Englishman's inheritance from *Romana pietas*, fared much better. It is not so much the loyalties themselves that people reject (for kin and country at least are still regarded with devotion), it is the effort and discipline required to serve them. For after all, might not Granny be happier (and much less trouble) in . . . one of those Places? Or why should Percy have to do his National Service when Jimmy down the road got off to go to college? Percy may not be as *clever* as Jimmy, but college or no college it's the same world for all of us. . . . As for the country's institutions, few people take the trouble even to find out what they are. I was once required to address fifty National Servicemen on the subject of the British Parliament, and was somewhat hampered at the outset when it transpired that only ten per cent of them had a workable notion of the difference between the Lords and the Commons. They were pleasant lads, most of them, and excellent to work with and command, but the nearest they came to political criticism was a mild grievance because all politicians were old men. If, finally, we search for loyalty to the country's gods, we find that the old gods of the countryside have had their sanctums covered by housing estates and that God Himself is used with reverence only in time of trouble or by those who belong to churches other than the Church of England—which alone is the proper institution for Englishmen of true *pietas*. And so to make my point plain: If the old loyalties are so generally discredited among the people, it is no good expecting the people to have respect for the gentlemen who still seek to maintain them.

This point becomes even clearer when we consider those aspects of gentility which derive from feudalism. The gentleman is under an obligation to bear arms, and time was when he was honored, and in some circumstances blessed, for so doing. But he will get little enough applause for his efforts today, because the military discipline to which he subscribes and which he enforces is now seen as profoundly "undemocratic"—not to mention that it "thwarts individual expression." In any case, we all have to do our military service if called upon, so what merit attaches to the gentleman for his readiness to volunteer? He has no call to be pushing himself in front of other folk. Nor can the gentleman even be at peace on his own land. A paternal attitude to tenants or employees is resented as "condescending," while all his efforts to run his own property in his own way will be continually compromised by unionists and bureaucrats. Whether one regards this as a good thing or a bad, the result is the same: Just as the gentleman has been largely discredited in his traditional pursuit of military honor, so he has been largely dispossessed of his traditional function as " 'squire."

Again, even the old Protestant ideal of individual conscience comes under fire. For while "individual rights" are now accorded almost hysterical attention, the sort of "right" referred to is that of being included in rather than that of opting out. To opt out, to take a different line, is to claim independence or even superiority; whereas what is required is that one should show respect for the "rights" of others by adapting oneself to their level. By the same reckoning, eighteenth-century standards of "style" or "manners" are deeply suspect; individual elegance of dress or idiom (as opposed to the wearing of mass-produced clothes or the use of a mass-produced jargon) is an insult to the tastes of one's fellows, and a skeptical type of thought or utterance is at once beyond their understanding and inevitably assumed to operate at their expense. (Of all forms of expression, irony has always been the most hateful to the uneducated.) Even common courtesies are uneasily received; for to put oneself out for people, even if it is only to open doors for them, is to imply that one understands their needs and has the power to minister to them (an attitude of condescension that sorts ill with ideas of "individual rights") and is further to suggest that one is superior in civility to others who may be present.

Last, we have seen that any inclination on the part of gentlemen to moral levity was firmly suppressed by the dire evangelical code of the nineteenth century—a code which, though its religious foundation has since been weakened by rationalism and indifference, still retains much of its moral power. But even this is now subject, in many respects, to a twisted interpretation: What was once a moral and individual obligation to be of service is now seen as a collective obligation to abide by the decision of the state; duty is now held to lie not—for example—in assisting the poor and the sick but simply in ensuring that one's own and one's dependents' Insurance Cards are properly stamped. Officialdom has replaced the gentleman in the sphere of good works, and so, for good or ill, has discredited him in yet another of his functions. In so far as the Arnoldian impetus to serve and rule still operates at all, it must now take the discreet form of "guidance" rather than the old form of direct leadership; for a leader is invited, as a matter both of duty and of honor, to walk in front, and no such precedence can be acceptable to the mean spirit of our time.

On the one hand, then, the notion of personal quality has been rejected, and with it the basic principles of gentility. On the other, as we saw in the last chapter, there is still much uneasy admiration of incidental wealth or luxury; while again, as we have seen in this, the overt privileges of merit excite the most acute and envious notice. Thus externals, whether they cause excitement or resentment, are in any case the objects of *emphasis*. The result is not hard to deduce: A man—any man—will now be assessed by surface or material standards. The old criteria of the upper class—visible prestige and lavish consumption—have now come to be accepted, in their most debased form, by the entire nation. For, after all, they provide such reassuring means of judgment. If you have two cars in your garage, then an immediately comprehensible estimate of your status can be arrived at, an immediate and comprehensible target for praise or envy is provided, and those who wish to emulate you are familiar with the terms of competition. But once let them be told that you are a man of probity, foresight, courage, or, worst of all, of genius—then they are up against unfamiliar qualities which they fear and resent and which all are therefore agreed to belittle or ignore.

And so the populace aspires to the baubles of the upper class, while the upper class still happily preens itself on their possession. Meanwhile, if anyone is still interested in the old and unspectacular concept of gentility, he will inevitably interpret it after the most superficial fashion. Overlooking the demands of honor and obligation, such a man will seek to gentle himself by the purchase of a small estate, perhaps, or by taking a commission in the Territorial Army. Dimly conscious that these activities are connected with the tradition, he will imagine that such an expedient makes him heir to the whole of it. Nor is this the end of the matter. Even those who cannot afford a farm or are unfit for a commission must be included somehow. True, the people have rejected gentility, but to make assurance doubly sure they must now all be "gentlemen" on their own terms. It is not difficult for them. All they need do, apparently, is to buy a secondhand British Warm, call the evening meal dinner, or patronize a roadhouse with a cocktail bar. Material standards, especially if you are not too fussy about quality, are very malleable, conveniently apt to render the measure of yourself which you require. But in all this, someone may ask, what of the real article? What of the gentleman who still retains the old standards despite the hostility of the times? What indeed. We had best revert to our friend, Captain Matthew Tench, M.P., and see what has become of him.

3

THE AGE OF BETRAYAL

WE LEFT MATTHEW TENCH in 1903, a newly elected Member of Parliament. The next twelve years were happy enough for him. His mother's death in 1907 was a blow, but it was an expected blow, the severity of which was further mitigated by the inheritance of her small but trim estate. In such circumstances it was desirable that Tench should marry, and married he was, early in 1909, to Penelope Golding, the twenty-five-year-old daughter of one of his new neighbors. Penelope was pronounced a charming and even accomplished girl with a hard core of good sense. Tench was prognosed as a considerate husband with an adequate if hardly dazzling career before him, the difference in their ages was thought to be suitable, and the union was allowed on all sides to be entirely correct. Its immediate fruit was two sons, Matthew and Peregrine, born in 1910 and 1912, and a daughter, Felicity Anne, born in 1913.

As for his parliamentary career, it was wagging along well enough. It cannot be said that Tench spoke very much (though a brief maiden speech on the Army Estimates of 1904 was kindly received), but he was conscientious, by the standards of the day, in handling the affairs of his constituents, affable to other members of all persuasions, thoughtful if rather ponderous in committee, uncritical about his party even to close friends and doggedly loyal to it in public session. He was thought of as a solid, unpretentious and on the whole capable member (no one thought of him as a politician) who would refuse the whip only *in extremis* and would never make an original suggestion in his life. It was also known that he was incorruptible; but there were those who averred (wrongly) that he would tolerate, out of party loyalty or herd instinct, at any rate minor degrees of chicanery. He was, in short, liked, respected, and, in the matter of his character and integrity, somewhat underrated.

For he had, despite a fundamentally conservative outlook (or possibly because of it), a definite streak of independence. Slow to recognize sharp practice (he had a generous nature and always gave the benefit of the doubt), he generally caught up with it in the end and then, by contrast with his earlier good humor, was unexpectedly and inconveniently strict in judgment. When, in 1905, a minor scandal of peculation had to be hushed up, he was anything but helpful; and he was curiously given to making blunt comments on the character and conduct of King Edward VII—until the death of that monarch, after which he never opened his mouth on the subject again. He was, too, slightly "unsound" on the question of the Upper House. He voted with his party throughout, but was once heard to remark, with unusual asperity, that it was idle for man to defend what God had clearly abandoned. Being pressed to expand, he deposed that hereditary government was morally defensible only when to inheritance were added competence and selflessness; in other words, the nobility might be well enough as a recruiting ground for legislators, for there would be less venality where there was already inherited wealth, but that a nobleman should be *de facto* a legislator was clearly not to be borne. However, such outbursts were rare, and it was generally held that Tench was a useful and modest man for whom, in time, a useful (and modest) place might be procured.

His private life was ample and seemly. He was happy in his wife and loving to his children—though neither his wife nor himself scrupled to leave the children while they took long holidays abroad. In the summer they would visit the Austrian Tyrol, in the winter they would spend some weeks in Italy. When at home in Wiltshire, Tench amused himself with the moderate pursuit of blood sports and saw to it that the estate and its dependents were properly maintained. While in London during sessions he would be joined, most of the time, by his wife, with whom he was proud to be seen about but whom he nevertheless deserted, at least two nights a week, for the masculine society of the Cavalry Club or White's, where he gambled for small stakes and drank the best wines with relish and temperance. Typically enough, he belonged to no club of prescribed political association; equally typically, he did not, so far as he could help, frequent the political circles of society. As to society, he was regularly invited to good houses though seldom, unless the occasion were one of state, to the greatest; this he neither regretted nor resented—indeed he was barely conscious of it—for he was, once more, a modest man and in any case did not lack for friends whose company he could seek with no other motive than his pleasure in it. Nor did he lack for entertainment: He tolerated his wife's fondness for the opera and shared her taste for the drama, while she in turn bore with his enthusiasm for such sporting events as the Eton and Harrow match, which he never missed if he could help it, and a certain class of race meeting where the emphasis was on the quality of the racing rather than on that of the spectators.

On the general issues of the day, his views were pragmatic and where possible kindly. Some years before, during the Wilde scandal, he had observed that the most discreditable feature of the affair was the desertion of Wilde by so many of his friends. He deprecated the hysterical procedure of the suffragettes, but allowed that their cause was just—though he would add, to tease his wife, that if women were to be granted equal rights, then they might also contract the corresponding obligation of paying for their own dinners. He regarded the Kaiser with distaste ("Never trust a man who preens himself in uniform.") but thought that his connection with the British Royal Family, if nothing else, should render him amenable as a party to negotiation and as an associate in treaty. He admired Winston Churchill, dismissing the Sydney Street affair as an unimportant escapade; said of Americans that they might be brash but were always hospitable; regarded income tax as sapping personal incentive; spoke of Haldane as a man of courage and foresight; and once inquired why, if Max Beerbohm was so talented, he should pride himself on being so unproductive. (He had a liking for Trollope at a time when his novels were almost unread.) All in all, his views were based on honesty, good will, appreciation of merit or endeavor, desire for others' happiness and a thankful acceptance of his own. For up to 1914 Matthew James Tench was a fulfilled and happy man, a man of assured if inconspicuous public place and well-found private establishment.

When the first war came, Tench was forty years old. But his place, as he saw it, was with his regiment. In vain did friends urge that he would be more use at home, that the swollen Ministerial structure of wartime would shortly offer many important jobs in which he might further the interests both of his country and himself; in vain did his wife plead and his brothers and sisters scold. For the trumpet had sounded in the ears of the soldier, and late in the day as it was he must saddle his horse and answer the call. Faced with this obstinacy, his friends set about to procure for him a War Office appointment that would sort well with his experience and his public position. Once again they reckoned without the character of the man. The trumpet, raising its silver note over an interval of fifteen years, had not called him to a desk but to the side of his old companions. To France he must go with them, and to France, in 1916 and after a frustrating period spent in training recruits, he duly went. At first there were tardy months in the rear, for things had changed since 1900 and there was now little place for the chivalrous panoply of spurs and saber. He wrote long and undramatic letters to his wife (in which, however, a certain relish for the sound of battle was to be detected), deploring the war but asserting its necessity, cautioning her not to expect an early end to it, hoping that all was well on the estate in Wiltshire, comforting and advising. But as time went on and men were ever more badly needed, the spurs and sabers were put away and Tench's regiment went into the line on foot.

During his fourth week in the trenches, the Colonel and his Second-in-Command were killed by a chance shell and command reverted to Tench. Shortly afterward his regiment was relieved. While Tench was on leave his command was confirmed, and the day after he returned to France he and his men were sent back into the trenches.

Thereafter, Tench's story did not differ materially from that of many other brave men. His rank enabled him to ensure for himself —or rather, enabled others to ensure for him—amenity just sufficient to protect the health of a middle-aged man against the terrible conditions of a winter in the line. In all other respects he shared every danger—every grief, every respite, every triumph—with the least of his men. As a disciplinarian, he was tolerant of all offenses save cowardice and bad faith. As a commander, he issued sensible and economic orders to achieve his limited objective—which was to stay put come what might—and set an example of cheerfulness and imperturbability in which there was nothing assumed or false and which, though it would never have inspired acts of high heroism, yet brought comfort to all in the dark hours and held them steady against attack. As a man, he let it be known that he regarded himself as being in the company of friends; and since he let it be known personally and even to the latest-joined trooper, to have betrayed Colonel Tench would have been to betray one's own soul. Mild, humorous, conscientious (but without regard to pettifogging regulation), humane, affable and unwearying, he went back and forth down the line with friendly words for novices and subalterns, sharing his flask with the sergeants and warrant officers whom he had known as troopers fifteen years before. As the winter went on he became known as "Colonel Mat" ("Seen Colonel Mat today? He told me his feet were playing up something horrible."); he was at once their commander, their mascot, their elder brother and their love. So that when, early in the spring, badly wounded in the knee and the groin, he went down the line for the last time on a stretcher, the men pressed around him like children, touching him shyly and wishing him luck, pressing on him little gifts of food and drink for his journey, and over and over again calling on him to come back.

But Lieutenant Colonel Tench, D.S.O., M.C., did not come back. His friends at home saw to that, and their task was an easy one. His wounds, for a man of his age, had been severe, his health, for all the care of his soldier servant, had not benefited from his winter's service. The authorities needed no prompting; Colonel Tench was fit for home posting only and might indeed be invalided out if he wished. But here his supporters grew cunning. All the best civilian posts had long since been snapped up by plausible stay-at-homes, and it would do Matthew more good, since he had started the war in uniform, to finish it so. They settled for three months' sick leave to be followed by a post in Whitehall which carried a certain romantic panache with it—a subordinate directorship of Middle Eastern Intelligence. The fact that Tench had never been east of Corfu and had no experience of intelligence work worried nobody, for even as late as 1917 they knew that his character as a gentleman would carry him through. And so Colonel Tench, a distinguished figure with his limp and his D.S.O., an exotic figure even, for he was now known to be connected with "spying," finished the war in great comfort and honor, both of which, God knows, he had earned well enough; but always, amidst the tinkling plaudits of the women he despised and the wary patronage of the men who had passed over his head while he was fighting, he looked for the better world which he, with his gallant company of friends, had suffered so much to bring about.

So that once the first gladness of peace had dwindled, the ensuing years brought little satisfaction to Matthew Tench. It seemed to him that the early twenties were years at once of hysteria and betrayal. The hysteria was that of those who had been too young to fight and yet somehow resented the fact of the war even more than those who had risked their necks or lost their limbs in it. The betrayal was far worse, for it consisted in a deliberate and politic evasion, by those who had once been loudest in their promises, of the obligations owed by them to those who had now—almost inconveniently, it would seem—managed to return. The hysteria of the very young, who had been children during the war (and often neglected children), was one thing; the treachery of those who had acted in the full maturity of their understanding was quite another. Not that Tench, conservative as he was, had looked for a New Jerusalem. But he had looked for a fair deal. Millions of men had demonstrated, in the most direct and affecting way, their unquestionable loyalty to their country; it followed, as an elementary point of justice, that their country should show gratitude in return, or, in plain terms, that those who had won the war should at least be properly fed now that it was over. But day after day, as the cries for help grew ever more desperate, they were answered only by the pulsing rhythm of the Charleston or, yet more distasteful to Tench, by the smooth denial and the friendly pat on the back which meant dismissal. For "times had changed," "things were different from what had been expected," and "we must all make sacrifices to the economic demands of the peace."

As for Tench himself, his material circumstances were still good. His income was worth less but at least it had not diminished. Even with three children to educate he could manage well enough—provided, of course, that he cut his domestic staff in two and went less often to Italy and the Tyrol. In Tench's case the betrayal operated in a more subtle way. It was somehow as though he were now redundant, unwanted—and the less wanted for the very things which he himself most valued, his experience and his past service. People found his point of view uncomfortable, "unrealistic," out of tune with the times. In Parliament, the men who had stayed at home and grown fat were listened to with respect as they theorized gravely and vaguely on the problem of the returning soldiers; while Tench's occasional plain comments which had to do with services rendered and stomachs waiting to be filled, were brushed aside hastily ("I know how you feel, my dear fellow, but you must concede that *my* experience in the *Ministry* . . .") or else were regarded as being coarse and indelicate, not in the best of taste. It was the same with everything in which he interested himself. Suddenly and mysteriously he had fallen out of step; he was out of touch, awkward, even suspect. But what could have happened? He was speaking in the same voice with which he had always spoken; he was speaking the truth, so far as he could determine it, and reasoning diligently therefrom. What, then, was this unknown quality for which he lacked? This "something" over and above truth, honesty and logic, this new and magical parliamentary ingredient the want of which apparently made all his efforts just an irritating irrelevance?

The answer was not difficult; and Tench, having with his usual good nature been slow to believe evil of anyone, yet finally grasped it. During the few years he had spent in uniform his world had changed: Before 1914 it had been inhabited largely by men who, stupid or narrow as they might be, were nevertheless pledged to serve their fellow men after the light of conscience and without any particular regard (for were they not substantial men in their own right?) to their own advancement; but now, in 1921, he was among men who had come to power or influence recently and on the tide of insecurity, who were therefore unconcerned with permanent values and thought mainly to help themselves to what was going while there was still some of it left. So this was the mysterious "something" which he was always neglecting in his suggestions— self-interest; not only was he not out for himself but he did not allow for the motives of those who were. It was a new climate, and it held no place in the sun for Matthew Tench. He was still considered a reliable party man, he was still regularly returned for his safe constituencey; but there was no longer any talk of advancement, however modest, for Colonel Tench—the returning soldier who had failed to move with the times.

And so, as the years went on, he occupied himself increasingly with country pursuits and in such backwaters of public activity as his colleagues were glad to leave open to him—ex-service charities and schemes for the employment of impoverished officers. The work was drab and demanding, and even country life afforded less solace than formerly. For here too Tench found his values were being disputed—this time from below. He was still respected, obeyed and even loved; but there was a spirit of questioning in the air, of mean and querulous questioning so it seemed to him, that rendered him uneasy and almost afraid. Why, the voices asked, were they all made to feel they owed so much to Colonel Tench? They weren't in the Army and no longer was he; and they had mostly fought in the war the same as he—and not got such pretty medals out of it. No doubt the land belonged to him and no doubt he was a fair land-lord; but were they also to be grateful to him because he had two sons at Eton, a well-dressed wife who was waited on by four serv-ants, and took a holiday abroad every year? By what right did he enjoy so much—less than before the war, of course, but still quite enough—while they were expected to touch their caps and thank him for enjoying it? Oh, no doubt he was a kind man, an honest man, who did his duty well and would come to their help at any time; but why should they depend on *him* for help? Perhaps if he and his kind had less, they would not need his help; not to mention those two sons of his, fine lads and friendly, but what had they done except take with both hands what their father gave them?

And so the questions were asked, and from time to time they were answered now, answered in a way that gave no comfort to Matthew Tench. But meanwhile the older people at least still re-turned his greeting politely and did his bidding promptly, so that in his private world he was not without reassurance. This was as well, for there was none to be had when he looked to the world at large. He had hoped much for the League of Nations because it stood for justice and peace; he had seen its ramparts crumble at the voice of the bullies, its champions depart at the least whisper of expedience. The war in Spain had confused him, and at first he had thought that Franco might after all stand for order and stability;

but he had then seen the evil men line up behind him and had come to understand, despite the protests of many of his colleagues, that decency and justice lay, insofar as there was either, with the forces of the left. He was therefore disgusted, not so much with the failure of Great Britain to oppose Franco, for even now he saw the quarrel as the internal business of Spain, as with its complacency and deceit. Communist Russia he regarded with as much aversion as he did Mussolini's Italy (what price now the memories of Venetian autumns, of the warm evenings in the Villa Borghese?) or Hitler's Germany; to justify the cruelty of the commissars on the ground that they served a noble ideal seemed to him the merest stupidity, to ignore such cruelty was hypocrisy of the lowest kind. Very bitter to him (he was always, in the last resort, insular) was the abdication of his King in the interest of private romance. Loyal to the crown itself, he had held indifferent opinions of those who had worn it since the old Queen's death; but even so, that one of them should have placed inclination before duty was incredible to him. The fact was here at least that there were still many people who agreed with him consoled him not at all. Over any issue, he would sooner admire—admire alone if need be—than recriminate in company. He had no relish for moral complaint; he desired now as always to honor and obey—and to deserve, for his own part, to be obeyed and honored. But what did obedience mean if a King could desert his people for the sake of a divorced and nameless woman? And what honor was to be had in a country where cowards danced hysterically in the streets because an old man with rabbit teeth brought back a piece of paper from Munich?

For Munich was the most bitter blow of all: It meant that England was now finally guilty of open and calculating breach of faith. And yet even those who did not revel openly seemed to regard it as sound policy. It will give us time, they said. Yes, but at what price? But could not he see, they said, that with things as they were certain sacrifices must be made in the cause of expedience? No, he could not see; he had never seen and he wouldn't see. Then the more fool he. And both from above and below the faces turned on him, a few with looks of pity for a lonely and perverse old man, but many more with looks of hatred for someone whose quality and strength of character shamed them all, casting the light of scruple full onto their smug and shoddy pretense.

Then came September of 1939. This time no trumpet sounded for Colonel Matthew Tench. The cause was to his liking, but he was sixty-five now, and would have been retiring from Parliament in a year or two had it not been for the war. As it was they pressed him to stay on and "keep things going." His career had been undistinguished, but his presence in the Commons after nearly forty years would lend a valuable sense of continuity, of normality, to the proceedings there. True to form, he still occupied himself conscientiously in the background of affairs. Although the work was as dreary as ever, it helped him to pass the days—and he needed help when the elder of his sons did not return from Dunkirk, when the younger was reported to have been interned by the Japanese. So Matthew Tench worked without recompense, advising and assisting in the formation of the Home Guard, a much-consulted member of local boards which had to do with agriculture, evacuees, conscientious objection, the peaceful billeting of soldiers. . . . And his wife girded herself to run the cold and empty house with the assistance of one decrepit charwoman, to organize Concerts and Comforts, to pacify the disgruntled and explain the new Forms and Regulations to the old women in the village, who somehow seemed to regard her as directly responsible for making them.

Nor did their burdens end here. For now there was a new spirit abroad, one which might have been detected years before but which only just now had come, almost overnight it seemed, to full and rancorous assertion. Tench first became conscious of it from the changed and swollen correspondence which he received as a Member of Parliament. Formerly this correspondence had politely posed harmless questions or sought some necessary advice; now it was virulent, accusing, sometimes anonymous; it denounced, it demanded, it threatened; and it was so worded as to imply that Tench himself was personally responsible for what it condemned, would himself be put on trial if this, that or the other were not remedied at once. The word "rights" began to appear in every line of it. By what "right," someone wanted to know, did Lord Warborough still get petrol to go in and out of Salisbury twice a week? Our Harry, conscripted three months ago, had been chosen as an officer's servant: Was he within his "rights" to refuse, and if not, why not? Mrs. Tracey (an anonymous letter this), being a rich woman, was hoarding tinned food and bribing the coal man. Miss Lodington had been whistled at by a corporal and wanted her "rights"; twelve-year-old Jeff Lawrence had been spanked by an officer, and his family wanted *their* "rights." Why were there still public schools? Why did officers get bigger rations than the men? (Our Jackie had done fatigues in the mess and seen them.) A Pole had made Brenda pregnant, and what were her "rights"? A Frenchman had raped Ada, and what was Colonel Tench going to do about it? Why did Colonel Tench travel first class to London, and wasn't third class good enough for all of us? Jack Peterson had won the M.M.: Why hadn't his wife received "the extra money"? What rations did the King get? If there was equal opportunity like the papers said, why didn't our Jimmy get sent to O.C.T.U.? And worst of all: We've had enough of you and your sort, Colonel Tench, and when the war's over we're going to settle you for good.

The harder he worked, the more reasonably he answered his correspondents, the more shrill the protests became. For all his efforts he was unwanted—tolerated as a scapegoat, exploited for his good offices, but at bottom unwanted and suspect. When he and his wife moved from the big, cheerless house (to which, as they now knew, Peregrine and the younger Matthew would not return) and into a vacant gardener's lodge, reactions were twofold: There were those who remarked with glee on the Colonel's change of circumstance; and those who complained that someone who could afford better should occupy what "by rights" belonged to a poorer family. When the big house was then taken over as a military hospital, resentment increased because of the "government money" which Tench was doubtless receiving. Nothing he could do found favor. And as for his wife, who did she think she was with her Red Cross uniform and her airs and graces? The War was all very well for her

because, you see, that sort liked giving orders and she hadn't got a
growing family to keep her busy.

They did not want Tench because he would not modify his character. They wanted to be reassured, flattered and provided for;
whereas Tench, albeit kindly and with courtesy, merely told them
the truth—that they must resign themselves to doing disagreeable
tasks and were in any case not qualified to dispute the necessity.
This was what no one wanted to hear. The papers said they were
a sovereign and heroic people; who was Tench to boss them about?
By what "right" did he give the orders—by what "right" indeed
had he been giving them all these years? He was no different from
anyone else. Oh yes, he had been about and knew a bit, but anyone
could do the same given his chance. And he was a brave man, they
said, and had worked hard all these years at the Parliament and
such. But Parliament or no Parliament a man was just a man, and
as for being brave, we're all made how God made us and needn't
think the better or worse of ourselves for that. . . . Little by little the
message began to reach Tench's ears. Voices grew louder, rumors
spread, his "good mornings" were answered churlishly, no one inquired after his wife. Little by little he began to understand; and
finally he knew that although there was much to be proud of in his
country and his people, although they had espoused an honorable
cause and would carry the day for it, yet part of that cause was now
to be rid of himself, for he himself, next only to the Germans, was
the Enemy. He must, he supposed, either change the principles of
his life and conduct or else get out of the way. He was not prepared
to make concessions, and the problem was only solved for him by
the end of the war. Now he was able finally and with good conscience to retire. He did not stand for the election of 1945. A young
man in a red beret, who said that officers and men were treated
exactly the same in *his* regiment, held the seat for the Conservatives
by a much-reduced majority. Despite his many years in the Commons, Tench departed almost unnoticed, with only a few—a very
few—old friends to buy him a melancholy drink. After the election
was over and the shouting had died down, he was awarded a be-
lated and grudging knighthood; and he settled to live for good in

the country (still in the gardener's lodge) and enjoy his few last years with his wife in peace and quiet. His income was much reduced now and pitilessly taxed; but he had enough to live with dignity and for an occasional bottle of decent wine.

I cannot think, however, that Sir Matthew was happy in his retirement. They had got rid of him all right, but he was still their butt. If things went wrong, he, in his retirement, was still to blame. If things were prosperous, then they congratulated themselves on having dismissed him and on their own skill in ordering affairs. In his old age he was either ignored, which he could endure well enough, or else beset with vengefulness, contempt and spite, which he learned, though not easily, to disregard. Either way his situation was unenviable. After a time he gave up trying to understand what motives were at work. For his part, he had told the truth, acted with good will, done his duty as he saw it, met his obligations, and remained loyal to his country, his dependents and his friends. He had feared no man, owed no man and cheated no man. His share of the world's goods, while ample, had never been excessive; he had used it widely and often generously; and he had yielded with a good grace when much of his wealth had been required of him. He had fathered two sons and lost them in his sovereign's battles; he had fathered a daughter and seen her well and timely married; he had known pleasure as a young man but he had not deceived his wife. If, then, people must find fault with him, his own conscience was clear; the reckoning would be with God, and he was ready to abide by it. But for all his dignified acceptance, he must have been lonely and sad. A lifetime of service, after all, was not something to be cast into a man's teeth like the dregs of wine at a quarrel over cards.

When Tench was rather over eighty, there occurred the Suez disaster. It was a story of mismanagement, broken faith and falsehood in high places. It signified the final and unquestionable end of his world. Nasser had acted highhandedly and without regard to contract, and had been acclaimed by two-thirds of the world for so doing; a Conservative British Cabinet, after a process of collusion worthy of a fifth-rate brothel keeper, had set up an ill-advised military action; the action had been bungled by incompetent generals and marred by indiscriminate bombing; several units involved had been disgraced by mutinous reservists, who had for years accepted substantial annual payments on condition of being ready to serve in just such a contingency; the country had been bitterly divided; the Prime Minister had been browbeaten into ordering a cease-fire just when something was at last being achieved; and those in positions of trust and honor had then conspired to spread lies about the history of the entire affair. Whichever way he looked, Colonel Sir Matthew Tench could see nothing but shame, crooked dealing and betrayal; and when, in the spring of 1957, he died one night in his sleep, he would, had he been conscious, have been heartily glad to be leaving a world which allowed neither credit nor place to his ideals or to himself.

So far this essay has been largely theoretical. Even the life of Sir Matthew Tench, though based on actual lives and events, is generalized—perhaps, some may say, romanticized—and in any case is so far of my own contrivance as to fit in rather too neatly with my own arguments. It now remains, therefore, that I should illustrate my thesis by reference to observed fact. For this purpose I propose to describe certain people and circumstances with whom and with which I myself have been well acquainted, holding as I do that in personal recollection, provided proper allowance be made for its limitations, is to be found the most vivid evidence of all. In my last chapter I shall also inquire after a remedy for the situation—for the gentleman has been of great service to England, we are much the poorer (though many would deny this) for his decline, and even now it may be that some new code, yet a code not wholly independent of the old, can set him up once more to guide our business and to do us honor through the world.

PART THREE

Illustration

Exiguus primum atque ipsos contractus in usus
eligitur locus . . .

Virgil, *Georgics*, Bk. IV, ll. 295–296.

DEO DANTE DEDI

IT HAS BEEN the contention of this book that the traditional gentleman, one, that is, whose life is founded in truth, honor and obligation, has been done down by certain hostile social pressures, envy
and materialism being paramount among them. These pressures
have compelled him either to abandon his standards of excellence
or, if he should retain them, to recognize that they are unwanted
anachronisms, objects at best of mockery and at worst of hatred. I
have undertaken to illustrate this thesis by describing people and
events in my own life. When due allowance has been made for the
law of libel, all that now follows is true. It has sometimes been
necessary to disguise a character's identity or to give an altered place
or date for a particular incident; but in either case the essential human forces at work and the essential nature of the circumstances
remain unchanged.

In 1941 I went as a scholar to Charterhouse. This prosperous
institution had originally been founded in 1611 for the benefit of
the poor—to educate its young and also, in this case, to give shelter
to its old. The founder, Sir Thomas Sutton, had been an Eliza-
bethan profiteer who had recourse to good works, since he hoped
to procure a place in Heaven as he had procured everything else
he wanted, by paying for it; so that the school motto, *Deo Dante
Dedi* (literally, "God giving, I have given") makes an apt use of
the present participle, which neatly implies that Sutton's gratitude
has future as well as past favors in view, that God's bounty is, after
all, continuous and so will continue to embrace Sir Thomas. But if

this motto may appear rather sly in respect of Sutton's original motive, it has since come to summarize, in the most honest and open fashion, the ethos of his school. For Charterhouse, whatever horrors it may have harbored in the eighteenth and nineteenth centuries, and however vile it may appear from the descriptions of Professor Robert Graves, is now a school which seeks to induce in its alumni ideals of conduct and service compatible with the good fortune they enjoy in going there. *Deo Dante Dedi*. In return for God's gift (Charterhouse) to them, the boys must give their services to their fellows and to God. Such is the school's unexceptionable doctrine.

But of course there are complications in all this. Sutton's original quota of a few poor scholars to be kept by charity has extended itself to six hundred boys of the middle and upper-middle class, most of whom are paid for by their parents. One may call this a "perversion" of the founder's intentions, or one may simply think, as I do, that the shrewd bourgeoisie has been quick to buy up a good thing for its own exclusive use. Whatever view you take, and whatever the rights and wrongs, the unquestionable truth is that Charterhouse has long been a school for the sons of gentlemen and that its ideal of service depends very much on traditional notions of gentility. This is far more true, I must emphasize, of Charterhouse than it is of Eton. For Charterhouse, with its City associations and its "business" founder, takes in the children of the middle and the upper-middle but seldom of the *upper* class (a nobleman at Charterhouse is a definite event); so that it is far less likely than Eton to suffer from the corruption and confusion of standards which result from fame and worldly acquaintance. In fact, of course, this means that Charterhouse is in many ways less tolerant and adaptable—less educative—than Eton; but it does enable it to concentrate, with less fear of distraction or sophisticated protest, on the formal moral training of its potential gentlemen.

But with all this, Charterhouse is not illiberal. Keen on "character" it may be, but it is not without regard for the cultural graces. This would not be readily apparent to a reader of Robert Graves' *Goodbye to All That,* in which he describes a school still spiritually dominated by a Victorian tyrant called Haig Brown; but by 1945 the influence of headmasters such as Robert Birley and of a staff enlarged and varied by wider educational demands had civilized the place to a point at which Professor Graves would have found it unrecognizable. One is reminded, now, that Charterhouse did after all educate Addison, Thackeray and Max Beerbohm as well as Baden-Powell. Again, since the school left London the City interest has weakened; Charterhouse no doubt turns out as many money-grubbers as the next place, but it no longer turns out more. The result of all this has been not indeed to turn the school into a paradise for sucking intellectuals but at least to place the emphasis firmly on preparation for the more liberal professions (the Civil rather than the Armed Services), to discourage any inflated ideas the boys may have about their future place in society, and to inculcate enlightened general attitudes to the world and what it contains. The boys are taught that it is no longer enough to conform with a class outlook; it is necessary to think.

In addition, however, they are also told that it is necessary to pray. And here we come to a vital and abiding element in Carthusian affairs. For Charterhouse was founded in the faith of the Church of England, and it is one of its statutory obligations to preach and enforce Christian doctrine and Christian morals. Please do not misunderstand me. It was not founded, as were the Catholic schools, to cater exclusively to one religious denomination, and it has no sectarian interests. On the other hand, it does require that its headmaster shall be a practicing and believing Christian of the Church of England, that his assistants shall not openly encourage atheism, and that all the boys shall conduct themselves in accordance with the strictures of St. Paul. Thus even the most moderate fornication is against the rules, not because it is harmful but because Christianity forbids it. Or again, while a Catholic in the school might be excused attending chapel in order to go to Mass, it would be no good for an ordinary boy to apply for exemption on grounds of sheer disbelief. Christianity at Charterhouse is an official necessity; now as in 1611 no one can openly opt out. God, by decree of the school authorities, is in His Heaven: a more tolerant God now perhaps than three hundred and fifty years ago, and certainly more reasonably interpreted in his demands, but there He is and there He will stay, and nothing you can do or say will remove Him.

The implications of this are considerable. On the one hand it strengthens the school's ties with the English tradition of gentility, for here if anywhere is *pietas* in action—in the form of unshakable loyalty to the most venerable of English institutions. On the other hand, and to say the very least of it, it does rather qualify the new liberalism to which I referred above. For the trouble about the Christian faith is that once you accept it you must also accept its claim to be the most important element in human existence and to provide incontrovertible answers to all human problems. The demands of Christianity are *massive,* its instructions beyond emendation or criticism. It commands that faith be set above intellect, virtue before intelligence; with the result that there comes a definite point at which rational liberalism must be discarded and beyond which doctrine must hold sway. So it is at Charterhouse. The new liberalism has done much to improve conditions; the boys are allowed considerable freedom and are treated with kindness and sympathy. But when the chips are really down, so to speak, then moral dogma prevails at the expense of enlightenment. Take sex. There is no longer any talk of damnation for masturbators, let alone of some hideous physical decline; it is now recognized that pubescent boys are bound to feel strong sexual desires and that so far from meriting reproof they must be given information and help; but in the last resort Christian bigotry is upheld, because if a boy actually translates his (theoretically excusable) desires into performance, with a girl or another boy, then he is still held to have sinned most grievously and he will pay the traditional penalty. From one point of view, indeed, the sinner is worse off now than he was in the old days of sexual obscurantism, for in the place of the old bleak silence occasionally punctuated by hell-fire sermons, there is now much "understanding" talk between masters and boys—talk which often leads to involuntary disclosures and so to one's own or someone else's detection. But be this as it may, the point, I think, is clear: The Lord thy God is a jealous God, and although He is less jealous than

He was He is still concerned to set definite limits to the application of tolerance and reason.

One must admit, however, that if traditional Christianity is in many ways the enemy of liberal progress, it also does a great deal to strengthen ideals of duty and service. It provides a firm frame of moral reference, and those who must undertake hazardous tasks, in disagreeable places and among unreliable people, may well need some such rigid support if they are to survive at all. It is all very well to talk of "character" or "personality," but very few people have much of either in the positive sense; the rest need firm and perpetual guidance (such as the Christian rule assuredly provides) to make up for their lack of resource, their poverty of intellect and their deficient appreciation of human motives—other people's and their own. Christianity (which did not start as a slave religion for nothing) will lend them the character they need: It will tell them who they are, where they are going, what attitudes they must adopt to those they meet, what labors are mandatory, what relaxation permissible, and (more or less) why. People of genius or even of exceptional talent do not need this information because they supply it for themselves; to them Christianity is an irrelevance. But there are few people of real talent and even fewer of genius, and of the six hundred odd boys to be found at Charterhouse in a given moment at least five hundred and eighty will need to be given a rule to work to. In which case, it may as well be the Christian rule. Christianity has its faults, but at least it keeps people out of trouble and encourages them to behave decently and often courageously. It is not at all a bad creed, irritating and absurd though it can be, for a school which prides itself on producing well-conducted gentlemen who are loyal to their country, respectable in their dealing, and who acquit themselves scrupulously in useful and demanding professions.

All of which brings me back to the Charterhouse at which I arrived in the September of 1941. I have used the present tense in the above discussions, but everything I have said is meant to apply quite as much to the school of twenty years ago as to that of today. In 1941 Charterhouse was ruled by Robert Birley, a man of enlightened views and refined intellectual tastes which were nevertheless conditioned, to a certain degree, by his deeply sincere belief in the Christian religion. This duality was also to be observed in many of his staff. Thus the climate of opinion was liberal, there was scope for individual tastes, the arts were held in respect; but we had Christian morality thrust on us in a big way, and, what was a great deal worse, we also had the war. This not only meant that the food was boring (it would have been in any case) and that much of our time was spent in grinding Corps parades or menial tasks "of national importance"; it also gave a violent twist to the boys' attitudes, exaggerating, at one and the same time, both the excellences and the defects of the gentlemen-pupils, both their readiness to serve and their fatuous assumption that their cause was the only cause worth serving. As was the case with everyone else during the war, the sense of crisis both heightened and concentrated all moral and social issues among us; just as socialists became visibly more socialist, lechers more lecherous, and good men more steadfast, so in our little backwater untried gentlemen became ever more conscious of the demands of gentility, developing and expressing attitudes ever more pronounced. I have often wished that I had been older at the time and better qualified to make a proper analysis. But at least I have some clear and often detailed memories; and since the scene should not go unrecorded, I shall now do my best to record it.

One of the least comfortable doctrines which prevailed in 1941 was that it was our absolute duty to prepare ourselves to serve in battle. The youngest boy in the school, who might reasonably have hoped that the war would be over before it could claim him, was expected to think in terms of fitness, alertness, suitability for future command. (The latter was not the least emphasized, because if it was a gentleman's duty to fight, it was also his privilege to fight as an officer—and an officer, what was more, in one of the better regiments.) The theory and practice of arms therefore played an insistent part in our lives, and an interesting (albeit extreme) instance of dedication to the military interest was to be found in a boy called Holtby.

Holtby lived only for the day when he would be commissioned in the Coldstream Guards. To this end he led the most rigorous life, scorning any activity which would not help him to it, and, since he was a person of authority in our House, he required us to follow his example. This was formidable. The First Holtby Law, on which all others were based, was that one should constantly toughen onself up by eschewing all sedentary pursuits and deliberately courting hardship. This meant lots of runs and cold showers, but was so far in the usual public-school pattern of things that it might have gone unremarked—had not Holtby now codified his demands so exactly as to penetrate to the very roots of one's private being.

The Second Holtby Law went into the question of games, for even he appreciated a change from cross-country running. To measure up to Holtby's standards, these must provide the minimum of pleasure with the maximum of stimulating discomfort and morale-building teamwork. In the winter football was Holtby's inevitable choice (unfortunately for him we were not a rugger school); fives and squash were dismissed as being namby-pamby and individual, while racquets, which required white trousers and expensive equipment, drove Holtby into something near frenzy, being seen by him as an affront to the whole national war effort. (Significantly enough, the authorities subsequently reinforced this view: Racquets, a costly and aristocratic game, was pronounced out of tune with the spirit of the times, and the courts were turned over, till the end of the war, as storerooms for emergency rations.) As for the summer, Holtby was much at odds with this season because it was decorative and warm; but he managed to get some of his own back by disparaging cricket (namby-pamby and individual again) and conscripting us into long afternoons of athletics, which, while also regrettably individual, nevertheless promoted disagreeable skills that would later be useful "in battle." Quite apart from all this there was a rider to the Holtby Law about games which held that whenever possible they should be replaced by parades of the school Junior Training Corps, thus making finally certain that everybody would be bloody miserable and the military cause correspondingly advanced.

So far, Holtby's activities were relatively harmless. There were, after all, adult masters to see that he didn't get out of hand. But the Third Holtby Law was insidious, and the more insidious because he could do nothing about enforcing it except to create and apply social pressures by his influence among the boys—an underhand procedure which might sometimes escape the notice of authority. This Third Law held that in time of war all mental activity was irrelevant and indeed unpatriotic, except insofar as it was applicable to the processes of warfare or was necessary to qualify one for a military career. On the Holtby theory, then, only science, geography and possibly modern languages were admissible subjects of study, and that people should use up the nation's resources, and occupy time that might have been devoted to the J.T.C., by learning history or Greek, was nothing short of an outrage. As for people who did extra work or read because they enjoyed it . . . well, it was Holtby's clear duty to remedy *that*. He might not be able to interfere with the school curriculum, but he could and did ensure that the spare time of "the intellectuals" was passed in a manner he approved—extra drill for "slackers" and the care and cleaning of our horrible J.T.C. uniforms. Furthermore, and as I have remarked, he could make use of social pressures. He was quick to broadcast his contempt for academic pursuits, found many sycophants to echo his views, and for a short time succeeded in making even the stronger-minded scholars feel guilty about impeding the war effort with their essays or elegiac verses.

But Holtby's real triumph was his Fourth Law, which had to do with the "House Spirit" and pronounced the good name of "the House" as the supreme end of all our lives. Conceiving our House as a regiment in miniature, he determined that it should become a model of conformity, zeal, fitness, teamwork and high moral tone, thus shaming the rest of the school and carrying off every available trophy. Any private indulgence or independent opinion was, of course, an insult to the Spirit of the House. Even School activities must take the second place (to the extent that House matches were made to seem almost more important than School ones); one must not have commerce with members of other Houses lest one should be corrupted by the laxity which prevailed in them; and one must on no account make frivolous or ironic jokes on such subjects (held sacred by the House) as P.T., God, Field Days, team games or sex. The result of all this was that most of us became priggish, interfering and petty; that we were cordially loathed by the rest of the school; and that Holtby, surveying a dining room full of shining challenge cups and obedient and tidy boys (in other Houses they were often dirty) was firmly and forever convinced that his system was right.

The impoverished lives we led under Holtby, the wretched values to which we must subscribe, will be aptly illustrated if I relate one farcical and wholly typical incident—the Annual Drill Competition of what was for some time afterwards known as "Holtby's Year." This event had been instituted many years before by some militant Old Carthusian busybody who had presented a cup which was to be competed for every December and on the following terms. Each House was to provide a full platoon, commanded by the senior cadet N.C.O. in the House, which would be drilled both by the judges and its own commander; a large proportion of the marks were to be awarded for the platoon's general bearing and turnout, the rest for proficiency at drill and the competence of the boy leader. The judges were normally drill sergeants from outside, often from Sandhurst, and so the Competition was also something more—an occasion for creating "the right sort of impression" and showing that the J.T.C. was "keen." By most of the School this Competition was very properly regarded as a tedious annual misfortune, to be approached with the minimum of preparation and contested with the minimum of effort. Downright mutiny was barred, because gentlemen did not behave in that sort of way; but the affair was treated, as indeed were most things to do with the J.T.C., with a defensive mixture of mockery and slovenliness which did some credit to the boys' sense of proportion.

But not in our House. Since the general standard was low, just a little energetic practice would have been enough to ensure victory; but Holtby was taking no chances and was in any case mindful that there were judges from the real live Army to be impressed.

No standard could be too high. Again, instead of selecting his platoon straight away and leaving everybody else in peace, he sponsored the widest possible distribution of agony by parading everyone in the House who was over fourteen and a half and only letting us go, one by one and with the utmost reluctance, when it became apparent that we couldn't or wouldn't do the House credit. "Couldn't" rather than "wouldn't," of course, because as I have explained our House was razor-keen and most of us would have found it unthinkable deliberately to flunk out. But I need hardly say that this is just what I did myself, being an unsatisfactory boy if ever there was one, and I was thus left at leisure to observe the increasingly bizarre performance of the crazed and hysterical Holtby.

After two weeks of practice parades, he had succeeded in paring his contingent down to the requisite platoon of thirty-two boys. Then, having only three weeks left, he really went to work. At every possible spare moment, in dark or daylight, out of doors or in, Holtby drilled his little band of men. When he wasn't doing that, he was practicing his word of command in front of a looking glass, at which time his wretched soldiers, supervised by one of his sycophants, were getting their uniforms ready for the great day. While the whole House rang with Holtby's parade-ground exhortations, haggard and despairing boys (who nevertheless remained keen to the last and spoke no word of complaint) pressed their trousers over and over again, polished their boots for literally hours on end, Blancoed their gaiters and applied Brasso to their buckles . . . Holtby himself, as might have been foreseen, got into a positively fetishist state about his own uniform. Being an Under Officer, the highest rank which the J.T.C. accorded its cadets, he was entitled to officers' privileges of dress. With unparalleled persistence and ingenuity, he succeeded in getting together (from masters, parents and even the school museum) the articles necessary to tog himself up in the correct drill order of a prewar subaltern of Infantry—Service Dress with Sam Browne belt, "plus-four" trousers with puttees and brown boots, and an endless finicking assortment of buttons and collar badges. (All this was happening after some years of war, and no officer had been seen dressed in this style since 1939 or ever would be again.) So that what with one thing and the other the dress rehearsal, which absorbed an entire half-holiday, was a memorable occurrence. Holtby, looking like the hero of a film about the Great War, bawled and bellowed his immaculate platoon through a series of intricate and rather beautiful drill movements time after time after time. If the smallest thing went amiss he stopped, practiced it until it was perfect, and then went back several stages in the program and started again from there. The exhausted platoon, held together as the afternoon went on only by their own pride and the unquestionable dominance of Holtby, hollow-eyed as they were and trembling at the knee, yet managed to remain steady and erect. Little by little boys from other Houses (who had practiced so sparingly for the Competition that they hardly knew there was one) gathered round to watch. With looks variously of amusement, pity, contempt, dismay and horror they lounged around Holtby and his dauntless platoon. But after a while, as the platoon wheeled and turned, advanced and retired and advanced once more, without a man out of step, out of time or out of line, the looks changed to those of admiration and almost of love. For there was something irresistible about Holtby and his platoon: they were ridiculous—and they were superb. And so when, at long last, the ranks were dressed and they were dismissed, a cheer broke out from the onlookers, a cheer which had much of irony, it is true, but even more of congratulation for the gallant performance of gallant men.

And of course, after spending the whole weekend repairing the damage done to their uniforms by the rehearsal, Holtby's boys won the Competition at a canter. They had more than three times the marks of any other platoon; their turnout had been faultless and their drill unbreachable; Holtby's uniform had caused a stir of regret for better days, his word of command had left the spectators speechless; even warrant officers of the Grenadier Guards had been stupefied by the expertise. But, as might have been expected, a deal of trouble resulted: Why, the judges wanted to know, was one House so splendid while the other nine just slopped around and giggled like a lot of silly little boys? The true answer, which could not be given, was that they *were* just silly little boys, but boys with a healthy instinct for preserving themselves, whereas Holtby's lot had been, in a way, the victims of the most monstrous personal exploitation. The official answer, which *was* given, was that Holtby was a boy of exceptional character and keenness, and that the slackness of the other Houses would be investigated. In fact, of course, the other Houses had always been just as slack and this had always, hitherto, gone unnoticed because there had been no Holtby to show them up. The judges had expected and tolerated boyish performances which differed only in degrees of ineptitude. But now they, and our own masters, had seen what could be done. In no time at all reproof and reform were everywhere; there was chiding, rancor, an end of *laissez-faire*; and our House, for all the applause it had earned at the rehearsal, was once again utterly detested, for it was the House exemplified by the unspeakable Holtby, the lean and hungry man who allowed his comfortable colleagues no peace.

But I cannot dismiss Holtby on this note and without a few more words. First, then, I shall likely be asked how I can possibly claim that the climate of opinion was liberal when all the time Holtby was being allowed to rampage around like a dragon. The answer is that Holtby was an extreme case, that anyway he was only one boy in one House, that his rule was brief because like all boys he grew up and left, and that, in fact, his tyranny did not go unnoticed by members of the staff. He was cautioned and he was watched; and if it be complained that he was nevertheless allowed to make life miserable for thirty-two boys for several weeks on end, I can only reply that it is as well for boys to learn fairly young that life is not one long round of pleasure—that disasters like Holtby crop up pretty frequently and must either be evaded or endured.

Secondly, I should point out that Holtby did not act out of malice and that his own advancement was only part of his motive. He did really believe, poor, stupid Holtby, that it was his duty to foster, in himself and others, those qualities and only those qualities which are useful in fighting wars. Toughness, self-denial, responsibility—these won wars, whereas books and pictures and sitting on one's bottom did not. Poor, stupid Holtby indeed: He clean forgot that

even wars come to an end and that one must find means of occupying oneself thereafter. When he left Charterhouse, he was duly recruited into and then commissioned by the Coldstream Guards, and
later acquitted himself with great determination and courage: He
led what used to be called "a forlorn hope," carried the day with
it and was viciously wounded. Then the war ended and so, in a
sense, did Holtby's life. He came to see us in October of 1945—just
before I myself was expelled. He was friendly and very quiet; he
was also drained of spirit and hope. Yes, he said, his wounds had
healed quite well and he had been pronounced fit to apply for a
Regular Commission. The only trouble was that he no longer
wanted one. Even so early, the Army was beginning to settle towards peacetime soldiering, and Holtby had no taste for the intrigue
and backbiting, the futile entertainments, the endless paperwork
and attention to petty welfare which he foresaw that this kind of
soldiering would soon bring. So what was he going to do? Well, his
parents wanted him to go to Oxford, so he supposed he might as
well go if they would have him there, and then see how matters
turned out. . . . There was little resolution, little "keenness," left
in Holtby. He was hardly, one might have said, "a credit to the
House." Unobtrusively and listlessly he said goodbye. I met him
again by accident some three years later. He was still lifeless and
without hope. No, he did not know what he was going to do when
he went down from Oxford in the summer; he did not much care;
he rather thought his father was fixing up something in the city.
Poor, stupid Holtby. I have no idea what subsequently became of
him, but I hope things turned out well; for he was a man of honor
in his way, and he truly deserved that cheer which the onlookers
had given for him and his splendid boy soldiers on a gray and distant December afternoon.

Another good example of extreme behavior caused by the over-
wrought sensibilities of wartime was provided by a boy called
Tower. He was a sensitive and intelligent boy, about a year older
than myself, and subsequently won a scholarship to Corpus Christi
College, Oxford. As the choice indicates, he was somewhat puri-

tanical in outlook, much preoccupied with the finer workings of conscience, but he did not disdain the pleasures of speculation and the arts. Thoughtful, humane, gentle, tolerant of others' moral deficiencies despite the high standards which he set for himself, Tower was in every way the antithesis of the unrefined Holtby and did not come off too well at his hands. Nevertheless, he was so clearly a man of integrity and inner strength that no ruler would wish to be without his support; even under Holtby himself he had enjoyed minor standing, and the succeeding regime, which though considerably modified, still retained a distinct Holtbylike flavor, co-opted Tower in the full dignity of House Monitor. It is upon this really very commonplace circumstance that the following incidents turn.

Before Tower's elevation, it had been our custom to go for long walks together, during which we discussed literature and religion and deplored Holtby and his associates. I myself would use them as the butts of crude satire; Tower, having a finer nature, would charitably seek for explanations. We had already heard of psychology, and I do believe that Tower tried in all seriousness to excuse Holtby's behavior on the ground that his early toilet training had been amiss. But I need say no more of that. The point is that Tower and I were good friends, shared many common interests and were both of us, though for rather different reasons, opposed to the boys in power. I should add that it was my habit on these walks to smoke occasional cigarettes, while Tower, whose trivial role in the House hierarchy he found inhibiting, would go away for ten minutes to admire a view and affect not to know of my delinquency.

When Tower was made a Monitor, however, this happy state of affairs came to an end. He summoned me to his study and in a friendly but extremely grave manner made the following address. I must understand, he said, that in general his promotion made no difference to his friendship for myself. Equally I must understand that the demands of discipline and group loyalty came above friendship. Since he was a Monitor, it was unthinkable that he should ever again join with me in criticizing, leave alone in mocking, the local oligarchs—who were now his colleagues. And another thing. Hitherto he had compounded with his conscience to overlook my cigarette smoking because he had managed never to *see* me at it; henceforth such collusion must cease. There was a rule against smoking because it was bad for growing boys; in time of war it was more than ever essential that rules designed to uphold purity and fitness should be obeyed. He was a Monitor and he would exact obedience. So far then from continuing to ignore what he didn't actually see, he must now take *positive steps* to detect me and bring me to punishment.

I had expected some changes in Tower, but that he should virtually turn into a policeman overnight was too much. Was he, I inquired, not taking himself rather seriously? After all, his new appointment was of a not uncommon kind (there were about ninety House Monitors scattered round the school) and had involved no laying-on of hands. Flippancy, he replied, was vain. Other Monitors might not take their duties seriously, but he, Francis Tower, did. He had considered the matter in the light of conscience and, what was more, in the light of the present stricken condition of Europe and of humanity. He would not budge. So I said I would try to avoid embarrassing him by my peccadilloes, wished him luck in the state to which God had now called him, and left.

Thereafter poor Tower started to behave in the oddest fashion. Rightly concluding that I was unreformed, he could not rest for trying to catch me *in flagrante* with my cigarettes. Should he see me, from his study window, on my way to a cricket match, he would close his books, hurry downstairs, and tail me all the way to the ground, lest I should knock off *en route* for a quick smoke in the school lavatories. Should he hear that I was going out in the evening, to a film show or a school concert, there he would be, lurking at the boys' entrance, waiting till I had been gone twenty seconds and then scurrying after me in the dark. The pathetic thing was that when I arrived at the proposed function Tower would join me, wearing a look both of frustration and relief, and would talk to me throughout, in his usual friendly and perceptive manner, about the subjects we had always enjoyed.

Plainly this could not last. If it irritated me, it was wearing Tower out. His work was suffering badly. He was constantly interrupting it at a moment's notice to play Sherlock Holmes, and his program was getting disordered. But how was he to be stopped? His conscience gave him no rest and I knew very well that it was useless to argue with Tower's conscience. And then once or twice, as he must know, he had only been cheated of his *coup* by bad luck—in which case both his conscience and his sporting zest for the chase would have been newly quickened. What could one do with such a fellow? His scholarship examination was drawing near, and my very real regard for his interests, not to mention my own convenience, called for decisive action. After some days of thought, and of the unflagging attention of Tower, I finally hit on a plan.

This depended on two considerations: first, that Tower was a gentleman and I was not; secondly, that if his conscience could not be argued with it could nevertheless be bludgeoned. So I went to Tower and asked him whether he hadn't really done enough. It was all, he admitted, very vexing, but I knew his views and therefore knew that he could not give up. But supposing, I said, that I now swore to Tower, *on my honor*, to give up smoking, would he accept my oath and desist from pursuit? On my honor? he said. On my honor. And here of course I had him. For nobody as decent and sensitive as Tower could refuse to respect such an oath when it was offered by a friend. So I swore on my honor that I would smoke no more, and from that minute Tower gave up watching me and was free to get on with his work.

Meanwhile, I was left to the unrestricted use of my pleasures. For I never had any intention of keeping my word; the whole thing was a device, and I still think it to have been neat and justifiable. Tower, by accepting the word of a friend whom he charitably assumed to have some honor, in every way retained his character of gentleman and was also freed, with credit and advantage, from the blistering demands of his conscience. I myself had not jeopardized my character of gentleman, because I had no such character to sustain; I had pawned my worthless honor to help a friend and to remove a grave impediment from my life. So Tower duly won his scholarship and I, for the time being at least, went rejoicing on my way.

And now I am going to tell a love story, for which I make no apology as it contains much that is relevant to my theme.

In this instance love was inspired by a boy whom I shall call Alexis and had a surprisingly late flowering. I had known Alexis for three years. I had swept floors with him, said House prayers with him and played football with him. I had for a short time regarded him as a friend but had later quarreled with him about "keenness" (for Alexis—little Puritan—was full of House Spirit and formidably keen). I had gone on field days with him, boxed with him and thrown bread balls at him—all this I had done for three years without regarding him as in any way out of the ordinary, when suddenly, for no reason at all, I fell for him like a cannon ball from the ramparts.

It came as a revelation. One afternoon, being at a loose end, I went to the athletics field thinking to find someone to gossip with or somebody worth staring at. And then suddenly, carrying a javelin over one shoulder and a discus in one hand (oh, shades of Phaedo and Lysis!), with a blond forelock dropping over one eye and a light down on his upper lip, Alexis, proud, beautiful, unattainable Alexis, went stalking past to the high jump. I rose and staggered after him. A goggling, gaping, bewildered fool, I lurched after Alexis to the high jump, there to be greeted by him with a cold "You look as if you need some exercise yourself" and to fall foaming and fawning at his feet.

After I recovered from the first shock of all this, I pulled myself together and started to make sense. To bring Alexis to the right true end of love would be difficult and perhaps impossible, and indeed I was not altogether sure I wanted this, but at least I should and could insinuate myself into his good graces. Since the bombshell had exploded only a fortnight from the end of the summer quarter, time was short. Making a snap decision, I announced to anyone who would listen that I was turning over a new leaf and was henceforth going to brim with House Spirit and patriotism; and then, judiciously dispatching two birds with one stone, I broke my rule of years and enlisted for one of the summer farming camps run by the school to help the war along—the very camp for which I knew Alexis to be bound. This was a deft move, if I say so myself, because such very concrete evidence of reformation could not fail to raise me in the esteem of Alexis and those to whom he listened, and I had also ensured that the two Alexisless months with which I was faced would be broken by a fortnight in his company. So far, so good. But while a fortnight's pastoral felicity might be all very well, I must look farther into the future than that. What then was my ultimate object to be? And what my long-term plans?

The first factor to be considered was the character of Alexis himself. I have already implied that he was "keen," athletic, somewhat forbidding and more than somewhat of a prig. (The Holtby regime had taken very firmly with Alexis.) On the other hand, he was a kind boy at heart, courteous and unaggressive; and while he adopted unthinking and conventional opinions about everything, he was disposed to listen to what he was told. The trouble was, of course, that those who had hitherto had his ear had filled it with platitudes; for Alexis, though thoughtful, was not clever, and he had therefore stayed fairly low down in the school, at a level where the voices of enlightenment were seldom heard. If only, I thought, I can win a hearing for myself, much might be achieved toward his education and my advantage. As for his morals, I was inclined to suspect that these were based on an objection to "doing anything dirty" or "upsetting Mummy" rather than on deep religious conviction. He had been confirmed, but only because everyone else had been, and I began to hope that Puritan, after all, was the wrong word for Alexis —that what he was really concerned with was decent, wholesome and gentlemanly "good form."

The second factor in the affair was my own attitude. What was this, how formed and whence derived? Now, I do not pretend to come very well out of this story, but I am bound to remark that even the most corrupt of us behave with a certain sincerity when they conceive themselves to be in love. And so it was here. My attitude was measured against what I honestly believed to be the best possible frame of reference for such matters—the utterance and custom of the ancient Greeks. I had recently found out a good deal about this, and as I understood what I had read the rules seemed to be these: Love between two boys was not only admissible, but praiseworthy and even ennobling; such love was best when it was mutual, protective and loyal, with no intention to exploit; *but*, even though it should operate on the level of the mind and the spirit, it was bound to include a physical element, for physical beauty, admittedly not the highest kind, was yet something to admire and to be grateful for; and therefore physical intercourse between male lovers was to be tolerated, provided it happened through the desire of both and without loss of dignity to either. This, rightly or wrongly, was how I interpreted what I had read, and these rules would dictate my attitude towards Alexis; and when I think of some of the passages which I *might* have read, in the Greek Anthology and elsewhere, I cannot think I erred on the side of laxity. I erred radically against Christianity, of course, but this did not concern me; even as early as that I was ready to back Greek reason against "revealed truth" any day of the week.

From all this it followed that my final object must be to make Alexis love me as I loved him. By interesting him, being loyal to him, amusing him, by giving him ground for admiring my courage, probity and (to be gradually revealed) my unselfish love of himself, I must bring Alexis to love me—love me for my talents, my character, my bodily attractions and my charm. Then and only then, if he wished and only if he wished, would I go to bed with him. And this should happen only if he wanted it from love: not out of curiosity, drunkenness, good-natured acquiescence or incidental desire, but out of *love*. It would on the whole be better, though this was neither the only condition nor an essential one, that the invitation should come from him.

So far, I am tempted to congratulate myself on my high-mindedness. But when we come to the practical plans and methods, which were worked out with Alexis's character and foibles in mind, the moral level drops. What degree of deceit may be pardoned in a lover I do not know, but I certainly exceeded it. I have already given, as an example of improvisation, my hypocritical enlistment for a school farming camp. My long-term plans were similar in kind. I intended to use a certain originality of approach, to spice our relationship with a (calculated) degree of paradox and wit, and to employ such charms and talents as I did in truth possess; but basically my plan consisted in representing myself to Alexis as something that I was not—as a responsible and gentlemanly boy who shared his enthusiasms and moral tastes. Having won his trust and his love, I should then, little by little, introduce him to my "Greek" rules. It was, by any measure, a vile and treacherous scheme, and I can only plead that I was much disordered by love.

But however that may be, the scheme worked. Two weeks of agonizing labor at the school farming camp brought me recognition and approval from Alexis enough to double my infatuation. The following quarter, through the peaceful days of autumn and on into the bitter weeks of November, the same process continued; I ran cross-country for the House, was punctual at football matches, eschewed "unsatisfactory" remarks about the life we led—and was rewarded with Alexis's smile. We were often together now. Little by little he was beginning to accept and admire the character I was constructing for myself, that of the clever and hitherto dissatisfied boy who had now realized that cleverness did not excuse him from normal obligations and had determined to settle to a proper observance of local customs and interests. For my part, I began to appreciate the unfeigned merits of Alexis: his good faith, the slow but honest workings of his mind, his essential purity of spirit. There were times when I was so moved by these qualities that I was almost compelled to give up my deceit, to cry out, "I'm a fake, I'm a sham. You must have me as I am, faithless and randy, or not at all." But my courage was never quite up to it, for I was terrified of losing him. And of other losses that such an outburst might bring. For while my charade had been devised for Alexis's benefit, it was beginning to impress authority as well. To Alexis's favor was added the housemaster's blessing, and by the spring of the year, reborn in the House Spirit and cleansed (as it seemed) of iniquity, I was made a Monitor and had arrived at the peak of my repute.

Of the ὕβρις with which I then began to swell and of the subsequent νέμεσις which punctured me I shall tell later in these pages.
Here we are concerned with Alexis; and Alexis, blinded by my successes (for in March I had won a scholarship to King's and in May
I was given my School Cricket Colours), had not yet perceived the
deterioration in my new "character" which these successes were
bringing about. Indeed, for him at least I tried to retain the modest
and virtuous exterior which I had wrought for myself during the
winter. For a time I succeeded; and at long last, on the day the war
in Europe ended, Alexis declared his love. Late that night, after
the celebrations were over and we were going upstairs to the cubi-
cles in which we slept, Alexis took hold of my hand and held it
firmly until we reached our doors, which were opposite each other
in the same corridor. I had never been so crapulous with delight.
For Alexis, anything so unconventional—so "sissy"—could only be
an extreme gesture of affection and trust. We looked at each other
and parted. But then, two minutes later, he tapped lightly on my
door. "Come and look at the moonlight from my window," he
whispered. Was this the invitation I had so often dreamed of?
Sweating with apprehension, I crept into his cubicle. "I thought you
should see this," he whispered. "It is so beautiful." As indeed it
was. A magnificent moon was shining down on the grass court beneath the window. The empty basin of the fountain was filled with
moonbeams; the bulky statue of Sir Thomas Sutton was transformed into a hero or a god; the shoddy sham-Gothic of the "old"
School Chapel now held the mystery of Chartres or Milan. No, I
thought, this is not the invitation. Even if it is, it must be disre-
garded, for the unusual events of the day have intoxicated us, and
the invitation must not proceed from drunkenness of whatever
kind. This, I thought, is Alexis reaffirming his love by sharing something he finds rare and valuable; it says much for his taste and
more for his generosity. I took a long look at the hellenized Sir
Thomas Sutton (I never saw him in *that* guise again), squeezed
Alexis's hand, and went away to bed.

In the ensuing weeks our love prospered in innocence, and this
was the best time of all. There were long walks during which little

was said; long hours of cricket in the sun (oh, those white flannels and the faint, sweet smell of sweat); long evenings, in his study or in mine, while we sat, hand in hand or knee to knee, and pretended to prepare the next day's work. But little by little I was pouring the poison into Alexis's ear. By a series of hints I imparted the gist of my Greek rules and their relevance to our own situation. What was between us was well enough, but there could be . . . more. More? Yes; provided it came by mutual consent and without indignity, there could be more. But . . . but . . . he had always been told . . . Told by sour old men, I replied, who had rejected an earlier and sweeter wisdom. But . . . but . . . did I then *want* more? I did not know. Did he? No, yes, no; it was so difficult, he could not tell. And then, a few days later, he delivered himself into my hands. Would I decide for us both? he asked. Surely, I thought, all the conditions I had made for his protection and the protection of love itself had now been met. He loved me enough to ask me to decide. Very well, I would decide; let him now come with me to a place of which I knew. . . .

When we got there, Alexis was nervous and shy, while I myself, fearful of offending him (of being too "dirty" or "upsetting Mummy"), tried hard to be patient and gentle. But then, for the first time since my revelation the previous summer, I made a mistake. I looked at him with a look of lust. I could not keep it out of my eyes. That this, which I had coveted for so long, should now be mine . . . *mine*. But on the instant the thought came, it ceased to be true. For Alexis had seen that look; at some stage, as my eyes passed over his body, he had seen my look of lust and read into my thoughts. "No. No," he said in a bleak, strained voice. "I see it all now." Miserable and ashamed, he began to pull on his clothes. "I can't . . . won't . . . How could you have done this?"

"I only wanted—"

"—You wanted your way with me and you nearly cheated me into letting you have it." And then, head hanging and eyes sorrowing, he left me.

In this fashion did Alexis preserve, as they say, his virtue. But he had also preserved something more—his understanding. In the end, his integrity and truth had prevailed; they had enabled him at the last to see through my shoddy pretense, they had enabled him correctly and in an instant to interpret the savage look of possession which I had given. And yet he was a little hard on me; I *did* love him, and had he looked at my face a few moments sooner or later he would, I think, have seen much tenderness there. But it was too late now; he had seen the sign of Judas, if only for a split second, and such a betrayal he could not forgive. We still saw a lot of each other—in our circumstances could not do otherwise—and in a way he still enoyed my company; but now he knew me for myself, as an insidious, nonmoral and amusing boy whom he could no longer trust or love; and as, with gay and cynical finality, I threw the last remnants of my moral disguise to the winds, and as the extent of my deception became ever more amply revealed to him, his off-hand friendliness turned to the barest civility, civility to coolness and coolness, by the time September came round once more, to bitter and undisguised contempt.

Jews are traditionally given a bad time at public schools and those at Charterhouse were not exempt. But I sometimes think that our treatment of Jews, though contemptible, was a much simpler, a much more *honest* matter, than civilized adults, with their deep and gloomy talk of racial prejudice, would normally allow. The fact was that Jews received harsh treatment in a direct ratio to the "Jewishness" of their physical looks. The prejudice was not so much against a *race* as against an exotic or abnormal *appearance*, which was punished quite as much in other boys as it was in Jews; but since, for obvious reasons, most Jews tended to look un-English, the proportion of Jews who came in for trouble was correspondingly high. Now, while a prejudice based on appearances is just as ridiculous and harmful as one based on legends of usury or conspiracy, I cannot but think that in immature boys who are being reared after the fashion of a herd some such hostility is inevitable. It is, that is to say, an *animal* type of hostility and as such, though cruel and dangerous, it is at least innocent of preconceived malice. The trouble is that as boys begin to grow up they confuse different sets of values: Having, when very young, regarded Jews as "not like us" simply because they look foreign, they get into the habit of so regarding them; so that when they are older they still think of Jews as "not like us," but for reasons that are now moral or social since it is in moral and social terms that they are now beginning to think. With this in mind, I am going to give an example of anti-Jewish feeling which sprang from a typical transitional attitude. The Gentile concerned was still at the elementary stage of distrusting unfamiliar looks, but he was beginning to relate that distrust to questions of gentility and good form.

There was, then, a very talented boy a year or so senior to me and whom we shall call De Freville. De Freville was not only blessed with an alert mind and strong athletic aptitudes, he was also from a slightly higher social stratum than the rest of us, coming of a family which was both well connected and rich. At the time of which I speak, he held a formidable position in the school, which was enhanced by his appearances for the School Cricket XI. He was not, as it happened, a very good cricketer, but it was thought that he lent the XI a certain tone by his distinguished looks, and since there were one or two places which were difficult to fill De Freville was as good a choice as the next man—and indeed, because of his immense general prestige, a much better one. To him that hath it shall be given.

Another member of that year's XI was a Jew whom we may call Stein. Stein was a very much better cricketer than De Freville, being a clever slow bowler (De Freville was an indifferent fast one) and also a useful man to bat at number six or seven. The trouble about Stein was that he looked more Jewish than one would have thought possible. Had a malicious cartoonist wished to exaggerate all the conventional physical traits of the Jews and then lump them together in one appalling caricature, he would have come up with something like Stein. I should add that Stein was in every way courteous and well conducted, and enjoyed the reputation of being an excellent monitor in his own House and a most loyal friend.

As far as Stein's and De Freville's positions in the XI were concerned there was no cause at all for them to quarrel. Stein had an absolutely certain place and would get his Colours any day now. De Freville had a much less certain place, it is true, but this was no fault of Stein's, and well De Freville knew it. Indeed, so far from being envious of Stein for his cricket or even disliking him on less specific grounds, De Freville had always been rather fond of him. Though in different Houses, they were contemporaries and had been in the same form for a period; and I had often heard De Freville quote, with approval, some quiet comment that had been made to him by "Ernie" Stein. In what follows, therefore, there was no element of personal resentment or intrigue; the whole disgraceful business was, in a sense, conducted with the most scrupulous objectivity.

Although De Freville liked Stein, being impressed by his manners and his abilities, he was nevertheless conscious of his highly irregular appearance. A more civilized boy than most, and used to superior standards of sophistication and tolerance when at home, De Freville took no part in Jew-baiting. "Leave him alone," De Freville used to say. "He can't help what he looks like." But even De Freville *preferred* people to look Anglo-Saxon, and he made no secret of this—least of all in regard to Stein. "I do wish Ernie didn't look so awful," he used to say; or, to Stein's very face and with complete good humor, "If only, my dear Ernie, you didn't look quite such a yid. . . ."

"But I am a yid," Stein would answer with equal pleasantness, "Mrs. Stein's yiddisher boy, Ernie. Now you, Johnny De Freville, you look to me like the most frightful *goy*. If only, Johnny, you didn't look *quite* such a *yok* . . ." And so on. A good thing, really—getting it out in the open. But in the last resort it turned out to go a bit deeper.

One day I was standing with De Freville (and Alexis) watching Ernie bat in the nets.

"Slow but sure, that man Stein," said Alexis gravely. "Useful chap. Dependable."

We all made noises of assent.

"There's only one thing bothers me," said De Freville at length.

"Oh?"

"Ernie's a useful player," said De Freville, "and well worth a place in better sides than this. And he's a sport, old Ernie, and a chum. *But.*"

"But what?"

"In three days' time," De Freville said, "we play Eton. It wouldn't matter so much anywhere else, but at Eton they're rather particular. What are they going to think of us when they get a look at Ernie Stein?"

This remark was followed by a long silence.

"I see what you mean," said Alexis at last.

"So do I," I said shamefully; "but aren't they quite—well—tolerant at Eton? Too grand, I mean, to *notice* things like that."

"The sight of Ernie," said De Freville, "would strain anybody's tolerance. Once they got to know him it would be all right. But they won't have time. They'll just see him, and then he'll be gone, and they'll say, 'Oh my God, how could they have brought a thing like that?' It's too much of a risk to our good name."

"It's a risk we'll have to take," I said, "unless Ernie drops dead before the match."

"I've been thinking about this very carefully," De Freville said. "It's rough on Ernie and I hate doing it. But we *cannot* have him in the side at Eton. So I'm going to Fletcher"—Fletcher was Captain of Cricket—"and I'm going to suggest that *just for this one match* he leaves Ernie out. He can play him in all the other matches, and give him his Colours as soon as he does anything to talk about, but Eton . . . *No.*"

"I don't think that's fair," said Alexis stoutly. "I see what you mean, all right, but I don't think you ought to go as far as that."

"What will Fletcher say?" I asked, evading the moral issue.

"I don't know. But he'll have to listen to me."

As indeed he would. Everyone listened to De Freville.

So later that day Fletcher was taken on one side and the talk was long and earnest. But Fletcher was a man of metal. He was quite prepared, in view of De Freville's prestige and the dearth of talent, to have De Freville *in*; in no circumstances would he consent to have Ernie Stein *out.*

"He wouldn't budge," said De Freville that evening, "and I suppose from his point of view he's right. Ernie's a good player and we certainly need a few. But as for me, chums, I can't face it."

And so it fell out. Ernie went to Eton, where he was treated with the same exquisite courtesy as everybody else; but De Freville, though he played in the XI for the rest of the season and in the end was given his cap, was absent for the Eton match. He had, so he assured Fletcher, an unexpected but important appointment with his London dentist for an extraction which oughtn't to wait.

All the events which I have related above occurred between September 1941 and October 1945. Meanwhile, of course, my time had been steadily running out—a process which accelerated violently after the spring of '45. At this time, as I have said, I was at the height of my repute and achievement: People had not yet begun to doubt the reform which my passion for Alexis had occasioned, I had just won a Foundation Scholarship to King's, and I was set fair for a successful season at cricket. After some consideration it was decided, in the late May of '45, that I should stay at Charterhouse till the July of 1946. I was only seventeen and a half, the extra year would give my scholarship an additional poise and breadth and, yet more important, would finally stabilize my moral character; for apart from anything else I was now almost certain to be chosen head monitor of my House by the following January, and such a position would necessarily confirm me in habits of service and responsibility. My future was thus sensibly and tidily appointed for me; but at this stage matters were taken over by the injurious god Pan.

For even my love for Alexis and the outward improvement of behavior which resulted from it had not prevented me seeking sexual entertainment elsewhere. By the midsummer of 1945 I was right out of control. Drunk with my own success in all fields, I had abandoned my reformed character, save only in the presence of Alexis himself, and with each day that passed I became more arrogant and more reckless. Here am I, I said to myself and often to the world, a scholar elect of a famous college, a "Blood" (*i.e.* a successful games player) at a famous school, bursting with energy and curiosity at the beginning of a summer which has seen an end of war. There is only one watchword now—and that is pleasure. I will find it out and have it. Inflamed and justified by passages from my favorite poets, I roamed the fields at noon and haunted the evening copses. Nor did the great god Pan ignore his votary. I am grateful to Pan for that summer; as long as it lasted he really did me proud.

Somehow or other I got to the end of July without being found out. Suspicion was in the air, I knew, but nothing definite could be proved, and at the end of the quarter I left for the holidays overtly discredited only by a very poor performance in the annual examinations. But what could that matter to a Scholar of King's? And anyhow, I told myself (with some truth), I have done a lot of interesting reading which has conferred on me benefits more enduring than marks in examinations. One must discover the world, I said; the minutiae of scholarship could wait.

But before I left for the holidays I was warned—by the boy who was to be head monitor in the autumn. He was called, let us say, Peter Morrison; he was a decent, upright and kindly boy, reflective without being intellectual, shrewd without malice, flexible but where necessary stern. He was to leave at Christmas, whereupon, as it was even now supposed, I should inherit his office. But Christmas still lay many months away and Peter, in the kindness and justice of his heart, decided to make his own attitude toward me quite plain.

"There are some odd stories going about," Peter said.

"Oh?"

"Very odd. I don't go out of my way to listen to gossip, and I don't believe what I do hear, but I'm at least bound to notice that there *is* gossip and that it concerns you."

"Meaning that there's no smoke without fire?"

"I didn't say that," Peter replied steadily. "Only that gossip, true or false, is a factor in the situation. You are an important figure here, not only for your personal prestige but because you are enjoying official trust. If there is gossip about such a figure, there comes a time when it can no longer be ignored. In the interest of good order it must be refuted. Which means that it must first be investigated. You follow me?"

"Very clearly," I said.

"Well," Peter continued, "at the moment there is no need for investigation. We are all about to go away for two months, many of us for good. By September the atmosphere will have changed completely and in any case memories are short. But if, as the autumn goes on, gossip starts up again and goes beyond a certain point . . . What can I do?"

"Suppress it."

"Not without examining it. And if, Simon, *if* I should find some substance in it . . ."

"What would you do then?" I asked.

"I should not be able to protect you."

Thus, with scrupulous fairness and good sense, did Peter Morrison make his point. There had been gossip, it would be forgotten, let bygones therefore be bygones; but should new gossip start (probably reviving old memories as well), then it might have to be looked into; and if it turned out to hold some particle of truth, then Peter could not in good faith conceal it. I have dealt with his attitude at some length because it seems to me to be an interesting and significant compromise—the attitude of a gentleman, certainly, but a gentleman of a very easygoing kind. If necessary, Peter had said, facts must be ascertained and faced; but until it was necessary, until things had gone *too far*, one did not take the chatter of the market place very seriously. He had been, I fear, too rational, too tolerant; he was talking in eighteenth-century terms—"Let sleeping dogs lie." But we should both soon have cause to realize that the nineteenth century had left in our midst other and more insistent maxims of conduct, whereby sleeping dogs were apt to be examined for fleas, whereby one was bidden not only to face the facts of evil but positively and officiously to hunt them out.

The warning was well meant and well taken. And yet, I told myself, nothing can go wrong with *me*—the Scholar of King's, et cetera, et cetera. A little more caution, which the climate of winter in any case enjoined, and things might go on as before—indeed much bet-

ter than before, because as heir presumptive to the head monitorship
I should be in a splendid position to command my own way. I
therefore returned in September with my mind set on a course of
action that should be libidinous yet covert. But I found there was a
melancholy over the school. Pan's visits to England are confined
to the summer months; Pan had departed, the leaves were down, the
earth was damp. Farewell, summer. . . . Brightness had fallen from
the air, and such amusements as did come my way were grudging
and without joy.

None of which is really relevant to my story; for as it happened,
long before I could get the measure of that autumn and its sexual
possibilities, the blow fell. Outraged νέμεσις had knocked at last on
the gate, and the Chorus was even now beginning to mouth its
usual assortment of platitude, complacency and spite.

What had happened was this. Peter Morrison had not been the
only one to hear gossip the previous summer. Late but inevitably,
the talk had come to the ears of a certain master who, far from
sharing Peter's easy good nature, had at once determined to pry
and probe. He had heard the rumors too late to take action in the
summer, but the moment we reassembled in September (two
months had little effect on *his* memory) he went to work. Having
collected as many rumors as he could, he then dumped his horrid
bundle down in front of the unfortunate Peter Morrison, demanding that its contents be sorted and a process of purification be at
once begun. Peter had no choice. After a few days of inquiry he in
turn took up the repellent bundle and put it in the only possible
place—bang in the middle of the housemaster's desk.

Then began an intolerable three days of questions, tears and
doubt. The housemaster, kind but inexorable, set himself to find out
anything that had ever happened. Evil had flourished, and now he
must reach to the root and pluck it forth. The evidence he had
originally been given pointed only to incidents fairly distant in
time; this being so, he might at first have been prepared to keep me,
if no longer as a monitor, until the end of the current quarter. But
as the hours went on, as more and more boys were summoned to
tell their stories, the volume of my guilt swelled until it seemed to

blot out the sky. Long-forgotten follies and passions were uncovered, then more recent ones, and finally someone cracked wider open than the rest and confessed to a squalid little scene which had taken place the previous week. This was the end. It brought sexuality so close that it might almost have been sitting there between us like a dog on the housemaster's hearthrug. Sadly, firmly, objectively, the verdict was given. Not only had I yielded to lust but I had practiced the art of seduction—that, it seemed, was what was truly unforgivable. It was one thing to succumb in the heat of the moment, quite another deliberately to bring such moments about. I had purposefully sought pleasure; I had planned for desire. And then, I had broken trust. I had abused my position as a monitor, abused it as recently as last week. Surely I must see that there could no longer be a place for me as a monitor or indeed anywhere in the school at all. My victims, for so they must be regarded, would receive gentler treatment; but as for me, I must go. My parents were sent for to escort me home, my trunk was packed with the assistance of the goggling and gratified matron, and on a misty autumn afternoon I left my boyhood behind forever.

And so the ultimate sanction of gentle society had been passed against me. I had betrayed that society; I had defied its morality, perverted its honors and spurned its obligations. It had therefore cast me out and set, as it supposed, the eternal seal of outlaw upon my brow.

At this point an attentive reader might well inquire what, in this chapter, I have been trying to illustrate. This book, such a reader might say, purports to describe the decline of the English gentleman —a decline brought about by historical and social circumstance; but so far from illustrating such a decline, the author has just given a long account of people who recently lived and flourished by the code which he tells us is moribund, and who indeed enforced the code, in no uncertain fashion, at the author's own expense. The only person who sinned grievously against the rules of gentility was the author, and grievously indeed he answered it. What evidence of decline in standards can we possibly find here?

But the point is, of course, that Charterhouse represented an entirely unreal and artificial set of conditions. Certainly the arts and customs of gentility flourished there, certainly the old rules of trust and leadership obtained; but only because, in that very limited area, matters were so contrived by the school authorities that this should still be possible. As soon as the cherished alumni grew up and passed out of the secluded nursery to the waiting world, they were in for some very bitter surprises. Or again, take the matter of my expulsion. This, as I say, had been the ultimate sanction; I had been marked, in accordance with the old code, as outcast and unclean. The only trouble was that the world at large did not recognize the sanction and could not see the brand which I was supposed to bear. When people found out that I had been expelled from Charterhouse, they simply laughed. If anything the affair turned out a social asset, since it provided a funny story to tell after dinner. The conclusion was inescapable: The code under which I had been punished was now invalid, the substance only of mockery or regret.

With this in mind, I shall finish this chapter by remarking how the persons who have featured in it were disposed of by the wider world. Of the fate of Holtby, the warrior-prince, I have told already. He had been allowed to keep the illusion which he had fostered at Charterhouse for just so long as the country could use them to exploit him as superior cannon fodder. With the war over, there was nothing left for Holtby and he knew it. The new Welfare Army would need officers to coax their men unobtrusively from behind, not the sort of assertive and flamboyant figure who undemocratically displayed himself in front. Holtby was good enough, as he had been down the ages, to fight the people's battles; but he was no longer good enough to order them about once peace had brought them their "rights."

Tower and his outsize conscience went off to Oxford and thence into the Army to do their National Service. I have never seen him but once since, and then I had to listen to an epic of complaint. He reviled undergraduates who treated their studies as a mere means to juicy jobs; he was disgusted by the easy morals of some dons and dismayed by the bigotry of others; he was shocked, as a National

Service man, by the lewdness of the soldiers, the coarse humor of the N.C.O.s, and the indifference shown to all this, and indeed to everything else, by the officers; and he had a great number of tales to tell about how he had been cheated out of everything from a lance stripe to a college travel award by people who did not share his scruples in competition. Tower, of course, would always have found the world a difficult place, but the postwar world was driving him demented; for he just could not get anyone to understand that the law of *quid pro quo* is a moral injunction as well as a commercial one.

De Freville, always a worldly boy, was one of the few who was prepared for what he would find. I don't say that he liked it very much but he was ready, as he had been in the affair of Stein, to set his face and cope. De Freville knew early that certain sections of society take up certain attitudes; that Etonians may be polite to the Steins who come as their guests, but comment on them after they are gone. So De Freville, who had never been a gentleman in any case, went into the world to compromise with it. He remained on good terms with Stein; he was careful where he was seen with him. He inherited wealth and fulfilled adequately the office which his wealth imposed on him. I have seen him several times and I do not think he is happy. He drinks too much, he gambles heavily and rather boastfully, he is bloated to look at. He has compromised himself into a set of what one might call "Sunningdale" standards and people, realizes this, shrugs, and calls for another drink. He always knew something of the sort would happen and wishes it hadn't. De Freville will die young, unlamenting and unlamented.

Alexis—ah, Alexis—he sailed away to Africa. Since he had been educated to deal firmly and fairly with subordinate black men, all went well—until the black men started to want their independence. Alexis could not and cannot understand this. He is an official and not a settler, so he is not worried for his property; but he is bewildered and hurt that the natives should wish to change his own beneficent and equitable rule for some species of demagogic mismanagement. Charterhouse taught him to do his duty, and this duty he has done; it also taught him to expect ingratitude; but it

did not warn him of the impending and utter rejection of himself
and all his kind. So Alexis, all unprepared, will soon be exiled from
the life and country of his choice. I am not at all sure what will become of him and do not like to think.

Peter Morrison, amiable and tolerant, yet so disliked the world
he must live in that he eventually settled in the very heart of the
country and would not stir from it. Thus he kept his happiness, but
it was a limited happiness because it consisted in rejecting nine-
tenths of what life offers. Peter's routine domestic existence was
really another kind of death. He felt the cold wind, against which
Charterhouse had failed to clothe him, and he shriveled and shrank
away.

Mr. Birley, who had presided over us and encouraged us, with
all sincerity, in the illusions of gentility, took up an appointment in
Germany late in the forties. I don't know how he reacted to the
spectacle of a corrupt Control Commission and a roistering Army
of Occupation, but I cannot think he was gratified. Yet Occupied
Germany, while it was a contemptible scene of fraudulence and
lust, showed the way the world was rolling, for it represented the
plaguetime revels of an imperial class, which knew that its hours
were numbered and that the death carts were passing through the
street, and so, becoming bitter and false to itself in its defeat, was
cocking its last snook at the new ideas and the new people who
would destroy it. It was not a lesson for Mr. Birley to relish.

So that, in one sense, I myself came out of it all the better than
anybody. I carried no illusions into the world with me and, insofar
as it was then a vigorous, muddled and amoral affair, I found it to
my liking. The subsequent reforms of the Labour Party, the ever
more insistent demands of the collective social conscience, I found
sentimental and irritating, but for me they were a challenge to my
powers of evasion rather than the sore denial of social standing and
function which they represented for many of my contemporaries.
On leaving Charterhouse, I went into the Army, found no one
remotely shocked that I had been expelled from school ("for the
usual thing, I suppose"), and eventually went out to India in the
same platoon of officer cadets as Peter Morrison himself. We were

commissioned on the same day and spent our leave together in the hills. The outlawry which Charterhouse had sought to impose on me was meaningless. Partly because even Charterhouse came to see this after a time, and partly because of kind support from friends on the staff, the sanction was little by little withdrawn, and from 1948 onward my name was to be found on the list of recognized Old Boys. But that is by the way. The pertinent fact is that the boys I knew at school, insofar as they accepted and practiced the school's gentlemanly code of ethics, were all subsequently disillusioned and betrayed—betrayed most of all, in a way, by the failure of the school's sanction against myself. The times were against them; the tables on which their code was written hung around their necks and nearly choked them, made them conspicuous as targets of abuse and ridicule, cruelly hampered their withdrawal. Myself, on the other hand, by betraying the Carthusian ethos, had passed forever beyond danger of betrayal. No tablets of moral exhortation around my neck; I was left free to travel as light as I pleased.

2

THE SCAVENGERS

BETWEEN LEAVING King's in 1952 and re-entering the Army in the May of 1953 I spent most of my time in London. I did some work as a book reviewer and otherwise contrived to support myself by backing racehorses on credit—if I won, good, if not, then I borrowed money to refresh my accounts. It was an exhilarating and instructive period of my life, and the more so as it brought me into frequent contact with the kind of people and the kind of attitudes to which I have referred in Chapter 1 of Part Two ("The Age of the Gossip Column"). I was privy, that is to say, to the goings-on of several "upper-class" persons on their own ground; and if their way of life was enticing, I relished even more the spectacle of their pettiness.

Central to many of the people I knew was the engaging figure of the Honorable Susan Strange. Miss Strange was the daughter of a nobleman of very long lineage indeed; she had a substantial private income (from a trust administered by lenient trustees), she had a charm compounded in equal parts of perkiness, arrogance and blatant sexuality, and she had a brilliant if somewhat jerky intelligence which she exercised on the arts, literature and social scandal of the day. These interests made her ubiquitous: A cocktail party to celebrate a first novel, a straightforward society wedding, the preview of the latest film about Negroes, the opening of an oyster bar, the closing speech of a divorce case, the inquest on a Chelseaite who had gassed himself—none of these functions was complete without the attendance of Susan Strange. She was a robust, inquisitive, unself-conscious and entirely attractive figure whom everybody loved and longed to spoil. If, for a time at least, she remained unspoiled, it was not for the lack of the most debilitating attentions.

These came from two quarters: from the society columns of the gutter press, and from the sycophants who gathered around her, desirous of exploiting variously her social notoriety, her money or her lust. To do her justice, Susan was democratic in dispensing her favors of whatever kind; she would as soon bed with a Guardsman as with one of his officers, and she was just as happy with ravioli in a cellar as with *foie gras* in the Ritz. And to do her followers justice, it must be said that many of them were talented and genuine people who sought her company for its own sweet sake. But as the only time I knew her at all well, there was a top dressing of upper-class, or aspirant upper-class, admirers who, being in every way better provided for than other members of the circle and thinking very highly of themselves on this account, were determined to keep Susan as far as possible for their own exclusive use and never ceased to titillate their vanity by reminding each other of her birth, her connections and her *chic*. It is these latter whom I mean when I refer to Susan's sycophants, and it is in these who will concern us here.

High on the list stood Mr. Darrel Vesey. This was a lank yet personable young man whose father, a failing Norfolk landowner, had shored up the family fortunes by marrying the heiress of a lavatory manufacturer. Mummy and Daddy were now long dead, but lavatories are a commercial constant; so that Vesey had found himself at the age of twenty-one in command of money, land and also unlimited leisure, since it suited everyone that he should leave the management of the sanitary works to his mother's younger brother. After finicking his way through three years at Oxford and there developing a taste for the chatter and license of artistic circles, Vesey had decided he was cut out for the pursuit of literature. Knowing that many famous writers had expressed a traditional preference for the Mediterranean—and indeed that to be an expatriate in itself bestowed distinction—he had spent two years wandering from France to Italy and from Italy to Greece, maturing his thoughts as he went and paying expensive court to any celebrity who lay on (or within a hundred miles of) his line of march. He reported on them at length in his letters to his friends in London, and had slowly and cunningly fabricated an image of himself as a brilliant young man of promise who was recognized as such by the great all over Europe. ("Willie says . . . Robert says . . . Morgan says . . ."). He had further elaborated the legend by becoming, for a year or so, a combination of secretary, librarian and personal valet to a mangy but still reputable lion on the island of Cos. When at the end of the year the lion died, it was found that Darrel had inherited his money and, what he needed a great deal more, his esteem. For Darrel was to be the literary executor—a gratifyingly simple task as the old gentleman had written some twenty thousand words in the last twenty years. So Darrel Vesey had returned to London to arrange for the publication in one volume of the six wispy novels from which his benefactor's disproportionate fame derived; he had also wangled some sort of sense out of the few thousand words which survived in manuscript and had printed these at the end of the volume along with a brief "appreciation" ("to E.E., in memory of his unforgettable last year") by himself. The appreciation was full of words like "sensitivity" and "delicacy"; the volume was treated with respect by all literary editors because its author, while commendably left-wing himself, was also the uncle of a prominent shareholder in a right-wing weekly; and Darrel, who appeared at the publication party in dove-gray shoes and a black tie, was accorded the flattery and respect of all. Having thus justified his choice of career, he remained in London to enjoy his triumph— which he managed to eke out by writing ever thinner and more etiolated articles ("The Last Summer of E.E.," "E.E. on His Death- bed") for literary journals. It was at this stage that I first met him; he was then daily expecting an invitation to lecture in America ("E.E., Artist and Friend").

If Darrel Vesey, in seeking Susan's approval, had some claim, however perverted, to intellectual distinction, Martin Forsyth Browne ("Marty") had little to rely on except his money and a talent for effective spite. His recipe for social success was to find out the flaws in others' lives, and then to exploit these either to entertain or to blackmail—his price being not money but invitations or recognition. If he kept very quiet about the dowdy school to which his wealthy but mean father had deliberately sent him, he had a lot to say about the famous cavalry regiment in which he had served (with real gallantry, as it happened) during the war, and his even more famous college—where he had picked up a facile system of cultural cross-reference which, fueled by his natural ma- lignance, could be used to deflate any achievement on the part of others. (He never deflated Darrel Vesey, as they were nominally friends, and he acknowledged and respected the kinship of the spurious.) Apart from these destructive activities, which were very pleasing to his mediocre and vicious acquaintance, Marty won suc- cess by using his money to render his ambience in various ways unusual or spectacular, thus convincing those near him that they belonged to an exciting and significant circle which was the envy of society and the focus of public attention. Mean like his father before him, and having ingrained bad taste, Marty would provide only the most indifferent champagne at his parties; but it would be served from double magnums which were being kept cool in gigantic ice buckets with pornographic drawings stuck around them, and he would have had his flat so got up with six-foot candles and black velvet drapes as to give an impression of the "brilliant" or the "uncommon" strong enough to transform the third-rate guests into persons of imagined quality. Unknown to Susan, Marty would have rung up the press to tell them she was coming, and when the party was besieged by photographers he would once more be able to tell everyone how distinguished they were in their gaiety and way of life—"So sorry, my dears. I tried to keep this little do quiet, but they won't leave *us* alone for a minute." Gratified shrieks and murmurs. Such were the tactics and values of Martin Forsyth Browne, who, I should add, peddled insurance among his friends in order to turn a few extra shillings.

While both Darrel and Marty were young men, Susan did not lack for more elderly attendants. One of these was a middle-aged psychiatrist of vaguely mid-European origins who had inherited a tidy sum of money from his late wife and who, though he still claimed authority in medical matters, had ceased to practice and now occupied himself investing his wife's money in film productions. Arnold Reiffar, for so we may call him, had appointed himself as a sort of unpaid court physician to Susan. He waited on her assiduously, was always ready with interesting pills to buck her up or calm her down. In his wake there followed his stringy and whey-faced familiar, Sykes Mortimer, a man of about forty, who was rumored to have abandoned a brilliant career in the Diplomatic Service in order to live with Reiffar as a sort of secretary-*cum*-disciple. Wherever they were, Mortimer's anxious and almost doglike face of devotion would follow Reiffar round the room, brightening at his lightest utterance, becoming strained and impatient if Reiffar was crossed in the smallest particular, slumping into haggard jealousy when his master, as he so often did, left the room alone with Susan to tend her nerves or her flesh with some form of "treatment." They said Sykes Mortimer had a handsome private fortune which was unreservedly at Reiffar's disposal on the frequent occasions when his speculation in celluloid brought him into difficulties. However that might be, he was perhaps the only person present who asked no share of Susan; he was there to be near Reiffar, from whom, at times, he almost seemed to hope for a message or an evangel; and although his loyalty to his friend prevented him from being directly hostile to Susan, he treated her with a courteous indifference far more invidious than the most open contempt.

Although one might despise and even hate Reiffar, it was yet easily possible to see how he had won Susan's trust and had virtually enslaved Sykes Mortimer. For quite apart from his distinguished middle-aged looks and imperturbable charm of speech and manner, Reiffar did have a kind of authority behind his eyes—an authority halfway between that of the hypnotist and the professional seducer—which might well promise delights to the hopeful and even a gospel to those wounded in spirit. He was like a fake Christ, and although he used his gifts to trivial and ignoble ends he must be acknowledged as a man of some quality. Not so Charlie Drake, the amateur skiing champion who had half killed himself with gin; or Charlie's Hungarian mistress, Polly, with her jangling bracelets and whining voice. Not so Lord Warren, with his puffy cheeks and his housing estates in Sussex; or Miles Joyson, who ran an antique shop in Kensington and arranged interior decoration for his friends. Susan's sycophants were in fact frauds and fools of every kind in the book; and yet they were able, as I have said, to separate her almost entirely from her more genuine and disinterested acquaintance, who admired her for herself alone and were far more capable of supplying the wants of her sexuality and intelligence. What, one asked oneself, were the sycophants' motives in so doing? How did they succeed? And why did Susan permit this?

In answering these questions, I must first repeat that all the sycophants, however raffish and undesirable they may sound from my description, had a good claim to belong to the upper class. Their circumstances, their scope, their resources, their tastes, their *savoir faire*, and in many cases their birth had given them so large a share of the world's goods, if not of public influence, that they necessarily enjoyed high status—however uneasy and ill deserved. Thus Darrel

Vesey was rich in money and land and, temporarily at least, had literary repute; or Dr. Reiffar, again rich, was "in" with powerful film people (many of whom he brought along to flatter Susan); or Charlie Drake had moved, ever since leaving Cambridge in 1931, with a celebrated set of St. Moritz-Riviera playboys, and had served in the Brigade of Guards during the war. All these people, even if originally they did not belong to the upper class, would in any case have been absorbed by it, since the English upper class knows very well that money and notoriety in others are dangerous if allowed to remain outside. All of them had therefore been more or less accepted; and so, being upper-class themselves, they found it socially necessary, and vital to their self-esteem, that Susan should not defect from the upper class or embrace any standards, of evaluation or of conduct, that did not conform with their own.

Hence their motive in keeping her to themselves. Susan must be made to surrender finally to material standards which had to do with cars, dress, restaurants, smart holiday resorts, and social success—this latter consisting in doing down or outshining others by oral malice or personal display. She must, therefore, be kept away from genuine intellectual or moral influences (though always being given the impression that her amusements were in some sense "intellectual" or at least "artistic"); and the delights of the society in which she was to be confined must be shown to her at their most dazzling and most compulsive—however many of Dr. Reiffar's interesting pills might be necessary to prolong the illusion. This brings us on to the methods used by the sycophants to keep Susan of their party, methods which were, in the last resort, a series of conjuring tricks. One important role was played by Marty Forsyth Browne, who arranged his "unusual" parties, suggested other treats and entertainments, kept telling Susan and everyone else how smart and delightful it all was, and contrived for frequent publicity. Meanwhile, Dr. Reiffar must use his hypnotic charm and medical authority, should ever Susan grow refractory or skeptical, to keep her up to the mark, to comfort her in bouts of guilt or alcoholic depression, to induce for every occasion the right mental attitude. Finally, all together would combine to flatter the girl in terms which depended variously on her noble birth, her private wealth, her un-questionable beauty and vitality, insinuating that all these things made her outstanding in this particular milieu—and would somehow vanish like fairy gold should she ever think to desert it.

It was this flattery, I supose, which explains why Susan yielded to the tempters and stayed put in their world of airliners and night clubs. She was, after all, of the upper class herself, and its criteria and amusements could not fail to appeal strongly to her: How much easier to remain where she knew she was a success, with all these kind, soothing voices praising just those qualities in her which might go unheeded, or even be mocked, by her coarser and poorer friends . . . Yes, it was no doubt better to stay where ingenious Marty, talented Darrel Vesey, understanding Dr. Reiffar (never mind his awful friend Sykes) could take care of her and bring out the best in her without making disagreeable demands of her effort or intelligence. So stay she did; but every now and again she showed signs of regret or rebellion, and it is one such incident, illustrating as it does the worthlessness of her captors and yet the efficacy with which they held her captive, that I propose to relate here.

One way of providing Susan with freshness and variety, and also of keeping her away from injurious influences, was to see she went frequently abroad—though only, of course, to the "right" places, to Paris or New York rather than to Athens. When she went, she was always followed by a handful of her sycophants, who ensured she met the smart people and received the correct brand of reassurance. In February of 1953 she announced her intention of going to Venice. The sycophants went into conclave, decided that Venice was suitable for her, though they were a little uneasy that she wished to go there at such an unfashionable time of year, and gave the scheme their blessing. Several of them then dropped all other plans and declared their intention of coming too. Susan professed to be delighted, and finally set out accompanied by a strong bodyguard which consisted of Darrel Vesey, whose invitation to lecture in America had not matured and whose literary acclaim in London was now running thin, Marty Forsyth Browne, who had jettisoned several promising insurance deals in his terror of being left out, Dr. Arnold Reiffar and with him the inevitable Sykes Mortimer.

In typical fashion, they all set up on the same floor of the Danieli Hotel. Darrel and Marty shared a small suite, while Susan, Reiffar and Mortimer together occupied a much larger one; thus they could all keep an eye on one another, and Reiffar would be immediately available should Susan require a therapeutic massage. It was suspected that Marty, who in those days was still very much on the make, had thoughts of proposing marriage to Susan, and so it was more than ever essential that no one should be left alone for a single instant; but in any case, whenever they came on such expeditions they all spent the entire day together since otherwise they would have been both bored and scared out of their wits. For to each of them the only reality in Venice or anywhere else was to be found in their own group and the few other people there of like mind and existence. Thus Venice for them *became anywhere at all*—which was what they wanted. They did not want to live in, still less to examine, an individual and beautiful city—which might have given Susan retrograde ideas. Venice to them must be, at the most, an unimportant backdrop to the essential business of being "smart" and outdoing others and themselves in material trifles; they might accept such anonymous features as the city had in common with most other cities they knew (the Gambling Rooms or "the best restaurant"), but the Basilica or the Piazza were menacing reminders of a force which, alien to their chosen world, might at any moment strip them bare of their pretensions and expel them naked into the night. Luckily, however, this was February, so convention did not require them to enter the Piazza even for a midday drink.

For a week or so, then, they all remained snug inside the Danieli, cosseted and self-satisfied, affecting to despise the local delicacies and sending to London or Paris for such fads as "proper" smoked salmon or "real" French wine. Occasionally they went to the "best restaurant" or a famous night club (Marty, terrified of loss, succeeded in keeping them from the gaming rooms), but these outings were always by night, so that the real character of the city could not obtrude itself upon them. But at last their peace was disturbed. An American art collector of their acquaintance arrived from Rome, encountered them all at their midday session in the Danieli Bar, and asked them to dinner for the following night.

So far no harm was done. The dinner was to be in one of "the best" restaurants, the American was a wealthy dilettante who subscribed, very largely, to the conventions of their own set, and there was little enough chance of Susan being got at by noxious influences. Or so they thought. But at Harry's Bar, where they had been instructed to gather before dinner, things began to go wrong. Not that there was anything wrong about Harry's, which is an amorphous home-away-from-home for smarties of all nations; but it just so happened that the American dropped the name of a well-known painter whom he thought to be in Venice, and that Susan, who knew his work and admired it, asked with great enthusiasm that a meeting be arranged. Before Marty could change the subject or Reiffar divert Susan's attention to a new and exciting pre-dinner pill, the American was on the telephone. True to the hospitable tradition of his country, he was determined that no guest of his—a female one least of all—should lack for what she wanted. The painter (who was called Patrick Ley, and was currently the white hope of all the chaster critics and antifaddists) was engaged for dinner, it appeared, but would be happy to join them at their restaurant for coffee. Susan expressed gratification, her bodyguard became fretful and pettish, and they all climbed into a motorboat (driven by a mechanic in a gondolier's outfit) and roared away to dinner.

The situation was now grave. Here was Susan about to meet, at her own urgent request, a serious painter who not long since had given a highly praised exhibition in London and was famous for his personal charm and his ironic indifference to socialite activity. In all probability he had only consented to join the party because he was short of Italian currency; such people, as Marty said to Darrel in the lavatory, were always ready to exploit the rich however much they despised them. But such people also had an eye for Susan's beauty, and if Susan took a fancy to him there was no knowing what might happen. She would certainly want to sleep with him, she might even go off with him and return, if only briefly, to the unsatisfactory world from which they themselves had rescued her. It was time to close ranks. The bewildered American host, who had looked forward to sitting next to Susan at dinner, was elbowed out of the way and nearly out of the room; and when they sat down Darrel and Reiffar were on each side of their protégée, while Marty and Sykes Mortimer (who alone was enjoying this predicament) were firmly anchored opposite her. She was being guarded in depth; now let this painter—Lee or whatever he was called, had anyone ever heard of him?—do his worst.

When, two hours later, Patrick Ley appeared, he was three-parts drunk but very articulate. He plonked himself down by his host at one end of the table, called for a flask of red wine, and launched into an informative but deafening lecture on the brushwork of Tiepolo. Susan's guard, exchanging disdainful and rancorous glances, drew their chairs ever closer toward her. Then Susan got up and marched out to the Ladies', gently declining Reiffar's offer to help her find the way. As she returned, she spoke quickly and smoothly to a passing waiter, who took her chair from between Darrel and Reiffar and set it down behind and just to the right of Patrick Ley.

"Who told you—?" began Darrel lividly to the waiter.

"I did," said Susan firmly. Then, tapping Ley on the shoulder as she sat down, "I've always wanted to meet you," she said, "and I've got lots of questions about your work." And for the next half hour she had eyes and ears for nothing and nobody but Ley. She ignored any attempts to distract her; the only refreshment she accepted was an occasional gulp of wine from Ley's own glass. Her followers squirmed in their seats, exchanged hissing remarks about "drunken nobodies," and finally started talking in significant voices about going on to the Cinquanta Club, a place of entertainment where they sometimes concluded their evenings. Still Susan took no notice. Finally Marty could bear no more. He pranced around the table, leaned over his host without a word of recognition or apology, and almost shouted at Susan:

"Are we going to the Cinquanta?"

"I'm not. Anyway not yet," said Susan.

"Sensible girl," said Patrick Ley. "Bad whisky and ridiculous prices."

"I wasn't talking to you," snarled Marty.

"And I wasn't talking to you," said the painter, "you dismal queen."

"Now, now, boys," said Susan. And then softly to Ley alone: "Go on telling me about Cellini and his mistresses."

"I *won't* be insulted," shrieked Marty.

And with a heave and a flounce he came up behind the painter and caught him a ringing smack over the ear. Ley retaliated with a glass of wine in Marty's face, the waiters looked dubious, the American host perturbed; meanwhile, Reiffar and Darrel saw their chance and took it.

"This is no place for Susan," said Darrel.

"Come along, Susan," said Reiffar.

And before she properly knew what was happening, Susan was in a speedboat hurtling toward the gaming rooms on the Lido.

"They'll never guess we've gone there," said Darrel, "except for Marty perhaps, and he's too mean to come near the place."

"Anyway we don't mind Marty."

"No, not Marty. Only those puffed-up nobodies who think that being able to paint or something excuses their hideous manners. . . ."

But although Patrick Ley had been beaten this once, he was clearly a menace for the future. Much later that night Susan was given a particularly soothing pill; a council of war was held; Venice was pronounced "dreary," with the assent of the somnolent Susan; and the next day after luncheon the caravan was on its way south to Naples.

I have devoted some space to these peripheral upper-class activities because they do seem to me to indicate, if only indirectly, the worthless values which obtain through the upper class as a whole and which, as a result of upper-class example, are spreading throughout the country. True, the more central members of the upper class would prefer a rather more stately application of these values—would think in terms of "grandness" rather than "smartness," of exclusive social clubs rather than expensive *boîtes*. Susan and her sycophants had a residual air of bohemia about them which in some small part redeemed them. But in the end it all comes to the same thing. The Jockey Club or the Cinquanta—both milieux accord and are accorded prestige on a basis of modishness and material snobberies. Which being the case, both have much in common with a milieu dominated by the washing machine or the H. P. Morris; and all three milieux alike are at odds with the traditional and self-effacing canons of gentility.

And another thing. In the preceding chapter about Charterhouse, and in the one which follows about the Army, I have attempted to show that the true gentleman, although he may still on occasion come into his own, is always done down again by the hostile pressures of modern society. Susan and Co., on the other hand, without message or mission as they are, have largely escaped society's censure and are permitted, and even encouraged, to live their lives out as they will. Insofar as they know what they want, they both get it and relish it; and in this they have the people's blessing, because their standards are, at root, the people's—standards not of character or intellect but of possession and display.

3

SHROPSHIRE LADS

I HAVE SPENT two substantial periods in the Army, one of them while I was doing my National Service just after the war, and a second some five years later and after I had come down from Cambridge. It is the latter period which I propose to discuss here, because whereas in 1946 the Army was still in a state of happy turmoil, by 1953 the conditions which were to obtain in the "new" Army and the issues which would face its members had become tolerably plain.

In the early summer of 1953, then, I reported to the depot of the King's Shropshire Light Infantry, having been appointed, in the rank of lieutenant, to a Regular Commission by University Entrance. I knew nothing of the regiment, save that it was occasionally mentioned in Housman's poems, where it was referred to as "the Fifty-Third," the number it had borne under the old system of designation. I believed, however, that it was an old-fashioned county regiment, unsmart by "brigade" standards but held in esteem in its home territory, and of the kind which has performed, modestly and steadily, all the most thankless tasks in two centuries of England's wars. In this estimate I turned out to be more or less right. I discovered that the K.S.L.I.'s social standing was below the rifle regiments but above most heavy regiments of the line. In Shropshire, at least, its officers were conceded to be members of the gentry and were invited, when in England, to all the tedious functions from hunt balls to memorial services which the gentry normally patronized; and although few of them were men of much substance in their own right, all the regulars (though not all the National Service officers) had been to important public schools, and some of them could boast a vague country house in their family background. As for the regiment's history, it was crowded, typical and valiant: We had sacked Washington, guarded Napoleon, fought plague in Hong Kong and floundered in the mud at Ypres. It was in fact a thoroughly good sort of regiment to belong to—middle-class and petty-minded, to be sure, but friendly, well mannered and close-knit.

During the five years which I spent with the K.S.L.I. I saw service in England and Germany and action, of a kind, in Kenya. Looking back, I see one thing very plainly: The farther away we were from England, the more we resembled the traditional prewar concept of an English regiment. This is important to my theme and I must now expand.

When we were in England, the men were close to their families, close to the whole postwar apparatus of welfare and complaint, and were daily reminded of the egalitarian spirit of the times. In England they wrote to their M.P.s, demanded compassionate leave if their mothers broke a little finger, heard much talk of strikes and protests and "the demands of youth"; and they therefore resented their officers, who, exercising as they did an arbitrary authority against which there was little appeal, clearly represented an older and altogether malignant order. Officers must proceed with great caution in England; any attempt to violate what people thought of as the citizen-soldier's "rights," any tendency to make him feel inferior, might at any moment bring into action the whole injurious mechanism of official inquiry and redress. (There was once nearly a complaint about an officer who sometimes wore riding boots; his servant disliked cleaning them and a corporal who did correspondence courses opined that they were "Fascist.") The minute, however, that the shores of England were left behind, the men started to become ever more dependent on each other and on their officers. They ceased to be civilians who wore uniform for eight hours a day and hurried home in the evenings to their mothers or their girls; they became soldiers whose only home was now their military unit. They were cut off in a little world of their own; if they wanted help or advice, then their officers were the only people who could give it. All talk of "rights" and "the demands of youth" was now irrelevant to the existence they were leading; for in order to be comfortable, in order, perhaps, to survive, they must knuckle under and accept the traditional and almost absolute authority which in England they had so much detested and which so many people had even told them was wicked. Gradually, as they discovered that this authority was in most cases exercised with good will and restraint, they learned, not indeed to love it, but to find it curiously reassuring. Their destinies, uncomfortable as they might be, were in the hands of officers whom, on the whole, they could trust. The officers in question were often stupid, conceited, snobbish or downright lazy, but the one thing everybody knew was that even the worst of them would never consciously betray his men. As the world runs, this was no mean consideration.

And so, while the men would much sooner not have left home in the first place, since nevertheless they must come they accepted with a good grace the discipline and even the social assumptions of an earlier time. Temporarily at least they were prepared to take officers at a much higher evaluation than in England—they were prepared to see them as their rightful leaders and even to allow that they were in some sense superior beings who were entitled to respect and privilege. In a word, officers were once again thought of as "gentlemen," and once again began to conduct themselves as such. They expected to be deferred to and obeyed, and for the time being they were.

But of course this state of affairs was highly artificial—at least as artificial as the conditions which, at Charterhouse, had similarly permitted the rules of gentility to prevail. Furthermore, the process was graded. In Germany, England and welfare were still quite easy to get at, and the men's dependence on their officers, and therefore their compliance, was by no means complete. In Kenya, on the other hand, they were so far away that mothers, M.P.s and the *Daily Mirror* were meaningless; and when they were finally in action the enclosure in which they lived had become absolute and unbroken. In action their officers reigned, without protest or qualification, as the paternal gentlemen-leaders whose word, being the only law available, was the only law their men knew.

Needless to say, an officer who let this power go to his head could make for very bad trouble and endanger the security of the whole artificial set-up. But this was rare, I'm happy to say; and it is more to our point to consider the reverse process of the one which I have been describing. The steps were easy enough to follow. First, the men gradually became more familiar with the strange country they were in; even though they spent much time in action, they still learned something of the people and the customs and slowly began to realize that here too there was a world outside the Army. This led to a slackening of their loyalty to their officers; for if there was an-

other, a "proper" world here, then there were other laws and authorities; there might even be people to protect them, just as there were
in England, people whom they could approach to demand their
"rights." After all, Kenya belonged to us, didn't it? Unceasingly if
almost imperceptibly the rot spread. After a year in Kenya the men
were back at what I might call the middle or "German" stage of
acquiescence. After a year and a half they were in something very
near an "English" frame of mind—sullen, resentful, intractable; and
had not some dramatic alarums and excursions intervened, sending
many of them packing up to the Persian Gulf, their attitudes might
have deteriorated still further. But in any case, their return to England finally brought them full circle. Back in the English midlands
they heard once more the half-forgotten watchwords of Welfare
and Equality, realized that no one could "muck them about" for
long, wondered how they could have been so far bamboozled as
nearly to have reverenced their officers in those distant days on the
troopship or in the forest. . . . Anyone who found the bonds which
had been forged there difficult to break was sharply chided by a pos-
sessive mother or a skeptical fiancée. In the midst of his praises for
Captain So-and-So, for his skill as a leader and his character as a
gentleman, he was abruptly told that there was no use for such as
Captain So-and-So in *this* country—that his sort was finished and
good riddance. Leader indeed! And be boggered to him for a "gentleman." What did our Willie think he was at, coming home and
spouting "gentleman" at his mam? And so the last traces of love
or respect faded, and the officer was once more only the class enemy
with the haw-haw voice.

It is this round process, from contempt to loyalty as we moved
away from England, from loyalty to indifference as foreign conditions became less strange, from indifference back to contempt when
the soldier finally returned home, which I take to be a symptomatic
feature of our age and which I would maintain reinforces the lesson
I have drawn from Charterhouse: That gentlemen can now only
behave as such, or be tolerated as such, in circumstances that are
manifestly contrived or unreal. I shall now tell of some officers who

did indeed come into their own in such circumstances—and of how rudely they were awakened by reality.

One interesting example of this pattern is to be found in the experience of a close friend of mine whom I shall refer to as Captain Wiley. A product of postwar Sandhurst, Wiley was a thoroughly competent professional officer, conscientiously concerned to keep his men in good trim and at the same time to save them unnecessary chores and vexations. While in this respect he was typical of the new Regular Army, in others he was more old-fashioned. He totally rejected the democratic view that soldiers, being individual human beings, must be treated with a certain reverence for their dignity as such. Faced with a group of ordinary privates, Wiley would assume, unless and until the contrary were demonstrated, that they were all wholly incapable of thinking, acting or arranging their lives in any reasonable interest, were not himself or someone like him present to guide and control. His attitude was essentially paternal: Unless people did what he told them, they would get into trouble, get into debt, get lost, get drunk, get clap, get killed, or in some such way make a bloody nuisance of themselves. He liked his men, he studied their individual peculiarities, he was sometimes even indulgent to them; but he could not take them seriously as adult and autonomous persons.

I shall not argue the merits or otherwise of Wiley's view, beyond saying that when one has to do with teen-age National Servicemen such a view sorts well with observable fact and answers usefully in practical situations. But this sort of thinking is not popular in our time, and it followed that Wiley was much disliked, in England and even in Germany, for the close patronage and control which he exerted. His men, quite naturally, felt that it was their "right" to make fools of themselves if they wanted to and in any case resented Wiley's assumption that they would inevitably do so if he let them. Although (or because) he was proved to be correct on an average of once a week, this resentment became only the more bitter.

But when we set sail for Kenya, the case was altered. The men now needed Wiley's protection and knew they needed it. They immediately accepted him as the father figure which he proposed himself to be. Later, after we had been in Kenya some three months, Wiley was given an appointment well suited to his intellect and tastes, and which incidentally concentrated his paternal attitude on to a very small human area. For Wiley, who was to be a kind of Intelligence-*cum*-Liaison officer, was now required to detach himself from our battalion and to live independently in a vacant farmhouse with a batman-orderly, a driver, and a sprinkling of black lower servants. Thus he became a kind of *pater familias*, having a household whose destinies he could oversee far more closely than was possible with a whole company of soldiers. And more than this: By the fortunes of war, he had been set up as a traditional gentleman in a traditional style of gentleman's establishment.

For a long time this arrangement worked excellently. Wiley enjoyed his Intelligence work and enjoyed governing his private staff. He was kind to them, saw that they had all they needed in their lonely outpost, was not too demanding of their services. At the same time, he made it clear to them that they must consider themselves dependent on him in a much closer sense than strict military rule required; for they must understand that he alone was now responsible for their welfare and safety in definitely unusual circumstances, and that they must therefore submit their daily lives to his careful advice and guidance. For their part the batman and (for a while at least) the driver accepted this as reasonable: They were both very young and in an entirely strange country, there were manifest dangers ranging from the bad drink sold by Indian storekeepers to ferocious tropical diseases, and it was evident that they could not cope with all this unaided. Clearly Wiley must be granted, beyond mere technical obedience, their absolute loyalty and trust. So Wiley was given what he asked and all, as I say, went well. I was invited to visit him at Christmas, and found a contented and well-ordered little group.

But as time went on deterioration began. In the first place, both the batman and the driver got to know, through Wiley himself, some of the local settlers and officials. They thus learned that the world around them was in many ways quite normal and hankered to exercise their own unfettered personalities within it. Furthermore, some of the minor and temporary officials, who were of a social class very little above their own, made scathing comments on Wiley's paternal rule and their submission. All this was already making for friction and bad feeling, when the batman, whose time had expired, went home to England to be demobilized.

For some reason to do with our battalion's strength and commitments Wiley was not able to replace the batman, but this did not trouble him, as much of the batman's job had in any case been delegated to the black servants. What did trouble him was the growing difficulty he was having with his driver. Egged on by his friends (mostly emergency "short-contract" men in the local police) to assert his independence, the driver was demanding more and more freedom—demands which Wiley, recognizing that the man now knew the country quite well, was on the whole disposed to allow. But matters did not stop there. The driver's parents in England, who had at first welcomed the news of their son's romantic situation and employment, now reacted with a sudden outburst of class paranoia: Their son, they felt, had been put upon; what was he doing out there in Kenya just driving one officer about all day long? They did not raise the question officially, but they wrote invidious letters to their son and spitefully incited a sense of grievance in him. He too began to feel put upon; it wasn't "right," it wasn't "proper," it wasn't "democracy" that he, a free Englishman of the working class, should be exploited as nothing more or less than a gentleman's personal servant. Being in the Army was one thing; everyone had to go through that; but being treated as a lackey was quite another.

In the middle of all this there was trouble from yet another source. When Wiley's batman had gone home to be demobilized, Wiley had suggested, since the boy expressed a hope to see more of the world, that he apply for a post on a planation in the West Indies —to assist him in which Wiley had given him a letter of introduction to a friend in London. To this friend the boy had duly gone and had successfully solicited a job. But this happy outcome had enraged his mother. The last thing she wanted was that her son, newly back from learning a lot of nonsense in foreign parts, should go rushing away again to more foreign parts. He should settle down, do a "real" job, court a "nice" girl, and fulfill his duty to his Mum —*i.e.* submit himself to her constant inspection and nagging. Foreign parts were immoral, to go there was an insult to family and working-class solidarity—an insult, indeed, to mothers everywhere —and it had all come about because of her boy's association with the likes of Captain Wiley. "Captain" Wiley, indeed! She'd give him "Captain"—interfering in all their lives with his letters and snooty ways. And so poor Wiley, instead of being thanked for his kindness, received three pages of illiterate abuse from a jealous mother, who also wrote and complained to our colonel. This second letter was so muddled and intemperate that it might have been accusing Wiley of almost anything from deliberate alienation of her son's family feeling to actual and personal assault. The matter was soon resolved, of course, but not without a great deal of tedious explanation.

Meanwhile, the driver's family, who lived near the batman's in the same town, got wind of what had happened and wrote a venomous and distorted version of it to the driver, whose demeanor thereupon became even nastier than before. Wiley, desperate, threatened to replace him. The driver, who underneath everything found himself very well suited by his unusual and interesting employment, had recourse to tears and promised amendment. He was forgiven, his services retained, and in an ecstasy of gratitude he wrote off to tell his parents how splendid and considerate an officer Captain Wiley really was. This was not well received. The driver's father, threatened, as he saw it, with the desertion of *his* son to a West Indian plantation, wrote to Wiley and demanded that the lad be returned to the battalion at once. Confusion was now so inextricable, tempers were so high and motives so low, misunderstanding of whatever he might do was so clearly inescapable, that Wiley saw only one course of action—he must apply, on his own part, to be replaced and transferred back to the battalion. This would surely cut the knot. But fate took pity and saved him the final humiliation of surrender. Overnight, half the battalion was summoned to the Persian Gulf; Wiley's area was no longer to be our responsibility, his appointment was honorably terminated, and with a sigh of relief he returned himself and his driver to routine and anonymous duties which would swamp the possibility of any future personal conflict. But he had seen and noted carefully the writing on the wall: He had been given the chance, and had taken it, to play gentleman after the old style—and had been roundly punished for his presumption the minute the world found him out. The moral was very clear, and he would not let it operate a second time at his expense.

A second officer whom I knew quite well figures in a series of events which, while illustrative only in the loosest sense of the principle which I am proposing, are nevertheless instructive.

One of a Commanding officer's biggest bugbears is the V.D. rate of his battalion. The old system of the quasi-official battalion brothel, with specially chosen and inspected girls, has long since been suppressed—thanks to the moral ardor of a public largely ignorant of the conditions in which soldiers must live. This gratuitous piece of interference has had its inevitable result: Soldiers in a country like Kenya, where there are not enough honest white women to go round, have commerce with native whores, and large numbers of them get poxed. Why anyone should ever have expected anything else to happen is beyond me; but it seems that both the public and the military authorities really do imagine that all soldiers are capable, on demand, of two or three years' complete sexual abstinence, their time being presumably occupied with reverent thoughts of their girl friends and their mothers. Regularly once a month, when the V.D. returns are sent up to G.H.Q., this ridiculous myth is exploded; but the authorities, instead of accepting what is clearly a law of nature and trying to deal with the problem in a sensible fashion, merely fly into hysterical rages and accuse commanding officers of neglecting their men's welfare and morale. When asked what, short of castrating his entire battalion, a C.O. is meant to do, the authorities mumble peevishly about physical exercise and healthy recreation. I suppose that they themselves must really know as well as anyone else that there is and can be no substitute for sex, but public opinion, and therefore official doctrine, blinks this particular truth because it is seen as unflattering to human nature. We live in a philanthropic age and must all think the best of one another.

So more and more exercise is ordered and more and more healthy recreation is provided; and when, at the end of the next month, the V.D. returns are bigger than ever, the authorities turn vindictive. Soldiers must be *made* to be chaste; sexual virtue must be ordained as a military command. At all costs the public illusion in the matter (clean and decent boys serving their country and sighing for home) must be maintained. Restrictions are therefore multiplied, more and more places are put out of bounds, the area is stiff with military police; about half the soldiers available spend their every moment preventing the other half from getting clap, and at last, amidst tremendous tension, some sort of control is achieved. One necessary condition of achieving it is that punishments for breaking bounds and so forth must be savage, much-publicized and rigorously enforced; and it is on this melancholy feature of Army life that the following story turns.

One of the best-liked officers we had was an aging and kindly man who was called, let us say, Major Stewart. He had long ago missed the bus, would never be promoted above Major now; but he was a sensible and experienced officer who ran his company smoothly. When we had been in Kenya about a month Stewart took his men off on detachment, to garrison a small village in the foothills of the Aberdares and thence to send patrols into the mountain forest. After this had been going on for several months, it was announced that Stewart's men, as having been the requisite time in action, were now eligible to proceed by batches on local leave in Mombasa. Here there was a leave hostel, bathing beaches, canteens, tennis courts, and a lot of other things especially designed for clean and decent boys serving their country and sighing for home; but there were also the traditional waterfront amenities, which no amount of authority or philanthropy had been able to disestablish. These, the holiday makers were told, must be avoided on pain of probable court-martial. It was, in any case, almost impossible to get at them, as they were virtually surrounded by a twenty-four-hour cordon of redcaps.

When the third batch of leavegoers returned to Stewart in the hills, trouble followed in their wake. It came in the form of military-police charges against two of Stewart's best men, who were accused of having been out of bounds together and having created a disturbance outside a knocking shop. The penalty for this sort of behavior was, as I have said, savage; and since there had lately been several such incidents, things were likely to go even worse with Stewart's men—it being a principle of Army justice that when an offense is "prevalent" the punishment must be sufficiently spectacular (the corpse rotting from the gibbet) to deter the most abandoned. In addition to all of this, both men were due to return very shortly to be demobilized in England, where they had excellent jobs awaiting them; their employers would not be gratified if they were delayed for weeks or months in Kenya while serving sentences in a military prison.

Stewart, in his bland, old-fashioned way, had never liked all the silly fuss about sex and V.D., regarding sex as a proper amusement for the young and V.D. as a tiresome but undramatic hazard. "Those who go swimming in uncertain weather," he used to say, "must expect to catch colds; but they will not find them difficult to cure." On general grounds, then, he was entirely behind his two men, and it was intolerable to him that their civilian jobs should be endangered because of a mere frolic. He was, of course, conscious of his duties as an officer; but weighing the matter, he decided that his obligation here lay in protecting two men who had deserved well of their country and in getting them off to the best possible start in civilian life. He was faced, however, with a considerable difficulty. While as company commander he must be the first to hear the charges against the two men, he was not himself empowered, since the charges were too grave, to give punishment in respect of them. If he found the men guilty, then he must remand them for the commanding officer, who would almost certainly request that a court-martial be convened. But there was one thing Stewart could do. While it needed the C.O. or a court-martial to give *sentence*, Stewart himself could arrive at *verdict*; if, therefore, he could contrive to find that the men were not guilty, he could dismiss the charges out of hand. That would be the end of the matter —for the men. For Stewart it would likely mean much trouble and explanation, as the military police are not fond of having their evidence questioned, least of all at low levels.

In this case, the evidence for the prosecution was in the form of signed statements. This gave Stewart a handle; for if the accused could plausibly refute the statements, then, since there would be no one present to shore up the prosecution by further argument, the charges would lapse. He therefore allowed the accused men to study at length the depositions which were given in evidence against them, and then invited their comments and their own version of the affair. The police deposed that the accused had been apprehended while standing outside a brothel in an off-limits area and shouting through an open window at the inmates. The men retorted that they had wandered into the area by accident, had been jeered at by three bawds from a window, had returned the salute, and had then hastened to get away. They had been stopped, they said, by a redcap at the end of the street just on the boundary of legitimate territory; the redcap told them he had seen what occurred outside the brothel and had then placed them under arrest.

Stewart, realizing that the truth probably lay somewhere between the two versions but not being able to see that any offense worth the name had been committed, questioned the accused at some length, finally accepted their explanation as being both rational and consistent, and dismissed the case. Then, with the help of a friend in "Q" Movements, he managed to arrange that his two men's names should be brought forward for passages to England a good three weeks before they were strictly due to go. This meant that before the military police would have had time to try anything else on (like bringing additional or alternative charges), Stewart's men would be safely out of the way in Shropshire. True, the military police had a long arm, but it should be possible to stave them off until the men had been finally demobbed.

Then ensued a rancorous exchange between Stewart and the military police:

Why had Stewart rejected the police evidence?

Because the accused had given a perfectly reasonable explanation of what the police alleged.

Why had he dismissed the case himself?

He was fully entitled to.

It was unusual if technically permissible; it was definitely disrespectful.

Disrespectful of whom?

The military police.

Pah!

Very well: new and different charges would be framed, and Stewart's C.O. asked to ensure that this time the accused were sent up before him.

Go ahead.

After an interval of a fortnight the new charges arrived at Stewart's fortress in the hills. He sat on them for a week, then sent them back to Military Police (Kenya) H.Q. in Nairobi, with the simple comment that the men accused were now in England and had been demobilized, as he believed, some two days before.

Why had he not returned the charges at once?

He had been on patrol and otherwise preoccupied.

Why had the accused been flown to England three weeks early?

They should inquire of "Q" Movements—or of God.

Why, when he knew fresh charges were pending, had he not warned the police that the accused had left Kenya?

He was not accountable to the military police for his men's movements.

And so on. None of this was doing Stewart's reputation any good, but worse was to follow. One of the men he had assisted broadcast his gratitude to Stewart far and wide as soon as he reached home and also spread a robust and exaggerated tale of the adventure which had got him into trouble. The affair came, via a disgusted local mother, to the ears of a Methodist minister, who wrote to a high-ranking officer in Kenya complaining that a major in the regiment which represented his own county of Shropshire was known to have connived in the immoral behavior of his men and to have protected them against its consequences. An important Shropshire personage (an old friend of Stewart's) visited the minister and managed to quieten him—but not before there had been much scandal spread and much offense taken. From being merely an internal quarrel, the Stewart business was blowing up for what the Army authorities dread more than anything—a public free-for-all. Stewart was summoned for high-level rebuke—he had put himself at odds with normal procedure, he had sabotaged the Army policy on sex, and worst of all he had nearly caused public outrage. What had he to say? Nothing, except that he had done his duty as he saw it. But poor Stewart had seen wrong, for he had seen through eyes which had not yet been adjusted to the perspective of our time; as a gentleman should, he had fulfilled his obligations to his dependents—but he had not allowed for the pressure of public opinion, which made nothing of loyalties such as Stewart's and saw his action as high-handed defiance of its morality and its will. The public wanted a chaste Army which owed allegiance to its homes and its mothers; Stewart had given them a glimpse of something they hated—an older Army, which cared nothing for chastity and which gave its allegiance to its leaders because these were men of trust and gave their own allegiance back.

In certain specialized circumstances, then, the Army still provides the gentleman with opportunities to behave and be accepted as what he once was. But, as we have seen, increasing pressures from without are making this more and more difficult; the opportunities are ever more rare and shorter in duration, the subsequent reactions ever more aggrieved. Nor can one honestly pretend that such hostile pressures come only from outside; for the Army is recruited from the public which crticizes it, and the values and prejudices of that public are therefore internally as well as externally applied, so much so that any officer who looks for a successful career must at least pay them lip service and is well advised, if he cares for his sanity, to bring himself to a genuine belief in them. (If you can't lick 'em, join 'em.) There are many ways in which I might illustrate the internal decline of the Army, and indeed much of what I have already said in this chapter has been relevant to this; but I think I can proceed most effectively by discussing modern attitudes to just two things: the marriages of officers and the recruiting of other ranks.

The traditional Army attitude towards the marrying of its officers was plain and logical. Domesticity could wait; the subaltern's business was to live close to his trade and so, by constant association with its fundamental elements, to acquire a deep and even instinctive understanding of it. Later, when he was better placed financially and was also professionally mature, he might seek his colonel's permission to marry the sort of woman whom his brother officers and their wives could welcome among them. But even then the Army and his regiment, that is to say his duty, must come before his family; and if he were suddenly required to leave his wife for a long time, then he might not complain and indeed would not have dreamed of doing so. Neither, to be fair, would she.

All this was well in accord with the view of marriage which prevailed in the upper-middle class at any time up to 1920. More recently, this view has been widely discredited in favor of popular and romantic notions which have to do with the sanctity of youth and love. The official Army attitude, terrified of affronting democracy, has changed to correspond with such notions. True, the Army Council declines to pay a marriage allowance before an officer is twenty-five, and certain regiments still keep up the fiction that the colonel's permission is necessary before an officer can marry. In practice, however, many officers both marry and are encouraged by their colleagues to do so in their early twenties. Everyone is indulgent to them. Cheap living quarters are found, they are excused irksome parades that might keep them late in barracks, they regard themselves as put upon if assigned duty on weekends. Indeed their duty and their comrades recede into the background of their lives, and whenever a battalion is to move, the first question is always, "What about married quarters? How soon can our wives come?" If the answers are unsatisfactory, there are sulks, threats of resigna-

tion, intrigues to be allowed to stay behind. Much rancor is expressed against those who are still single. "It's all right for you—
you've no responsibilities." "All you bachelors are the same—selfish
and restless. I suppose you're *glad* we've got to go to Hong Kong."
And so on. If a bachelor retorts that to get married is not after all
compulsory, he is told he is cold-blooded, antisocial, or, more probably, immoral. So the preparations for departure are bedeviled by
the complaints, absences and machinations of married officers, who,
in the end, are allowed their every whim; for the authorities know
that these days, what with "a young and lovely mother in Bucking-
ham Palace," domestic happiness is the highest social virtue.

Virtue, of course, is the operative word. Little by little the Army
authorities have been bullied into taking the lower-middle-class
view that marriage, even between the very young, is of itself a good
and virtuous proceeding. This view is partly sentimental— "young
love," etc., etc.—and partly moral—the more marriages, the less
fornication. But this dreary and righteous attitude reflects scarcely
a tenth of the self-satisfaction of the married couples themselves.
These apparently think not only that they represent a pleasing and
edifying picture but that by getting married they have somehow
done something very important in return for which society owes
them a debt of recognition. They think that marriage confers
prestige. "I'm a married man"—the speaker sounds as if he had become an alderman or been awarded the C.B.E. How often the telephone rings, with some newly married subaltern on the other end
of it: "I'm so sorry . . . my wife . . . perhaps somebody else . . .
Yes, I know it's inconvenient, but *you must understand that I'm
now a married man.*" Thus everything is thought to be excused;
complications and extra work may pile up for the company commander on the one hand and the platoon sergeant on the other
(themselves both married men, and with some right to be), returns and training may be ignored, the affections of the men alien-
ated, dinner nights with contemporaries neglected; but everything
is as it should be, because "I'm now a married man."

"There is no surer sign," says a character in Nigel Dennis's *Cards
of Identity*, "of the degeneration and collapse of an imperial class

than the need to bring the vice into the home instead of going out for it." And in the last resort early marriage springs from just that —from "the need to bring the vice into the home." What a thing to say. I know, I know. Marriage, quite apart from anything else, is a valuable social institution; it populates the country; it is recommended both by Homer and St. Paul. But what I am trying to point out is that marriage should come *after* a certain professional stability has been achieved, *not* at a stage when a man should still be living with the companions and learning the elements of his trade. Early marriage can be truly *vicious*, because it is so often caused either by pure sexual impatience or by an envious impulse to attain immediately to the privileges and establishments proper to older people. Before 1914, an officer who married very young stood to be accused of one or both of these motives. He might well have been made to resign first; he would certainly have been held guilty, if not of betrayal (as in A. E. W. Mason's *The Four Feathers*), at least of neglecting the Army's interest. For they would have said of him, with truth, that if he must have a woman then there were plenty available, and that it was the part of a gentleman to keep his assigned bachelor role in affairs, not to cause trouble and dislocation by premature nuptials. These days, of course, such an attitude would amount to heresy. The public wants—so the Army also thinks it wants— "lovely" young couples, steadily breeding in subsidized bliss, respectable, neighborly, unassertive, living only toward a pension and then death. The public does not want—and so neither does the Army—the old-fashioned type of officer who devotes himself, first and foremost, to a set of traditional masculine loyalties and seeks occasional relief in an excess of port after dinner or a visit to what Evelyn Waugh calls "The Old Hundredth." This of course is the type of young officer the Army *needs*; but first of all it lost the courage to say so and now, by a natural process of atrophy, it has forgotten that it is so. It therefore gets just the young officers it invites and deserves: They arrive at eight-thirty and leave at half past four, for all the world like clerks or shopwalkers. The few remaining bachelors, so far from being cherished, are given all the dirty jobs and regarded as selfish monsters if they are still unmarried at twenty-six.

In our own regiment, which was in some ways eccentric and even reactionary, we tended to resist this craze for early marriage. Up to 1957 we had very few married subalterns and even our captains were apt to stay single—a state of affairs which enraged the regimental wives, who conceived that their product, as it were, was being slighted. But we realized well enough what was going on in the regiments all around us, and even we were not totally immune from the virus of young love.

A symptomatic instance was that of a certain Second Lieutenant Barnes. This was an efficient and pleasant young man who came to us with a National Service Commission, had command of a platoon in Kenya, and then returned to the Depot in Shrewsbury to serve out his last three months before being demobilized. At this stage he suddenly announced that he would apply for a Regular Commission. Provided he passed the necessary central board, would the colonel of our regiment allow him to stay with us permanently? The idea was favorably entertained. Mr. Barnes had been at a grammar school, but, said the Colonel, we must move with the times; we knew him, we liked him, he had done well in Kenya; by all means let him stay. To this we said Amen, and started in a friendly way to learn what more we could of Mr. Barnes. For there is a great difference between having a man with you for two years and taking him on for life. Hitherto it had been enough that he could do his job and laugh or remain silent at the proper time. Now it would be nice to know something of his deeper attitudes and interests, since these might be important to us as the years went on. Everything, it seemed, was in order. Barnes had been to a reputable Shropshire grammar school, his father was a draper in a small local town (but we must move with the times, as the Colonel said), he was a good rugger player, did not care much for blood sports but held no "views," had no politics or religion worth bothering about, and could play the piano rather well. All this entitled him to our moderatae blessing—until the scandal broke.

Barnes was in love. Well, all right. With a childhood sweetheart from his home town. Hardly the end of the world. No, but he meant to get married early next year, *when he would still be a Second Lieutenant of only twenty-two.*

Meanwhile, Barnes had been before the Regular Commissions Board, which had very properly passed him. He returned triumphant, to be greeted by long faces. What was the matter? Well, had he, when he made his request of the Colonel, told him that he proposed to get married in a few months? No, he had not; at that time he had not yet been engaged. Then he had better go and tell the Colonel now, because it might make a difference. Make a difference? said the wretched Barnes; he had been promised he might stay, and that was all there was to it. Circumstances, we said, alter cases; in his own interest he had better see the Colonel, who would certainly want to see him.

So Barnes got on a train and went to see the Colonel. The old gentleman congratulated him on passing his board, repeated that he would be welcome to stay in our regiment, and then made discreet inquiries about Barnes's private affairs. Barnes had no money of his own, the Colonel supposed. No. That was quite all right, because few people had these days; but did Barnes have any encumbrances? Well, yes, he might have; he wanted to get married next spring. The Colonel drew a deep breath and started to explain: Regular Officers under twenty-five years old did not receive a marriage allowance; since Barnes had no private means, he would find it difficult to make ends meet and to join his colleagues in their amusements, however modest; in any case having a wife would make him less inclined to do so—at the same time as it would distract him from his professional business; all of which was highly undesirable. But, said Barnes, people in other regiments were getting married very young; he knew of two in the Artillery and one in the South Wales Borderers. But, said the old man, Barnes wasn't in the Artillery or the South Wales Borderers; he was in—or wanted to be in—the K.S.L.I. He had better return to Shrewsbury and think the matter over. Thereafter we had a difficult fortnight with Barnes. We went over the Colonel's arguments with him and pointed to other cases where early marriage had led, if not to disaster, to some awkwardness. If he was married at twenty-two, Barnes would be *cut off*: he would never, in a proper analysis, belong to the regiment at all; marrying at that age, before he had put down roots or formed proper connections, he would belong only to his wife. But he wanted to belong to his wife; that was what he understood marriage to mean. Yes, yes, but surely he didn't want to belong *exclusively* to her. Other regiments, Barnes replied resentfully, made a place for young married officers; why could not we? Other regiments, we said, provided a kind of accommodation address for young married officers; that was all. And surely, we said, he could wait three or four years would soon pass, there would be travel, excitement, *pleasure*—he would not miss a wife—and at the end of that time he would be sufficiently one of us to marry without losing his place among us. But Barnes was obdurate: Everyone was marrying young now, it was the right thing to do, this business of "belonging" was typical public-school talk, and as for travel, excitement, *pleasure*—what were such trivialities when compared with domestic integrity?

In the whole fortnight, Barnes would not budge an inch. At last the Colonel, mindful of his promise, said he might stay with the regiment, but remarked rather sharply that when Barnes went abroad there could be no question of a passage or accommodation for his wife—unless he paid for it himself. He would like to apply, Barnes retorted, for a home posting to the depot for the next two years; after all, a married man . . . He might apply to the devil, he was told; he was a young officer and would go where he was sent. Poor Barnes! He could not understand why we were so hostile to young love. Everywhere else, simpering teen-age pairs were being married off by the thousand and receiving nothing but applause and indulgence. Not, it seemed, here. But his story had a happy ending. He discovered, through some friend of his fiancée's, a regiment which resembled just one large and cozy married families' club; he applied for a transfer and was rapturously received by a host of pregnant young women who could not wait, they said, to welcome "his Phyllis" among them. Everyone, he wrote to us, was very friendly; but sometimes he missed our mess, because where he now was they hardly had a mess—only a sort of hut where the young married officers drank water with their hurried lunch. . . .

I have described this conflict at some length because the opposing pressures behind it are, I think, important. But I will elaborate them no further. It is enough just to add that even the K.S.L.I. and the few other regiments which have stood out against popular attitudes are, inevitably, beginning to yield: Subalterns are bringing home their brides and the old robust life of "the mess" falls daily into deeper disrepute.

The second symptom of the Army's internal decline which I have proposed for discussion is its attitude toward recruiting its regular soldiers. By 1957 the problem was already urgent. We needed a definite number of regular recruits in addition to our drafts of National Servicemen, and we were not getting enough. What was far worse, it was known that the National Service system was to be allowed to run down in the early sixties. We should then be entirely dependent on regular recruiting, and if we couldn't get even the limited number we needed now, what were our chances going to be then? Whether this problem has since been solved, and if so how, I cannot say. What I can vouch for, and what concerns us here, is the way in which the Army authorities and also the officers of my own regiment reacted to the problem some five years ago. Doubt, dishonesty, fatalism, false enthusiasm, genuine desire to do what was right—all played their part; and the outcome, which I shall now describe, is very relevant to my thesis.

Before 1939, the British Army was largely recruited from people who had not got enough to eat. They came into the Army for their meal ticket and, being in, made shift to lead tolerable lives. The Welfare State has stopped all that, and a good thing too you may say, but it has made matters very difficult for the Army. The only people now likely to volunteer are the very few who have a vocation for soldiering (most of whom go into some *corps d'élite*, such as the Guards or the Marines) along with the odd rolling stone who wants to put a distance between himself and a pregnant girl. This latter type can certainly produce good soldiers, but social mechanisms are now so highly developed that their pregnant girls (or whatever) are always catching up with them—which has an unsettling effect all round. For an ordinary regiment like the K.S.L.I., then, which had none of the glamour of the Parachute Regiment or the Hussars, the problem was how to persuade a working boy, who was enjoying good wages and union protection, to exchange these for discomfort, mediocre pay and an irksome form of discipline. At an optimistic reckoning, vocational soldiers and adventurous bad hats made up some fifty per cent of our needs; the other fifty per cent must be had from among comfortable and respectable young men, most of whom earned £10 odd a week and were courting steady girl friends. But how?

The War Office answer was that everyone must compromise. The Army would go some way to meet the recruit: It would pay a little more in cash, abandon the more obsolete of its disciplinary restrictions, give greater attention to welfare and individual needs. In return, it expected the recruit to give up a measure of his comfort and independence, pointing out that he could set against these losses gains such as travel, adventure and comradeship. The only trouble with all this was that it had no appeal at all. Travel, adventure and comradeship might be well enough (although I suspect that the lower classes are even more insular and domestic in their tastes than is generally allowed), but the brute fact was that Army discipline, whatever superficial changes might be made, must remain essentially the same as ever. An army, of its nature and function, must work by obedience within hierarchy; "take but degree away, untune that string," and you might still have quite an estimable organization for putting on tatatoos but you wouldn't have a fighting army any more. The man in the street knew this perfectly well, and so he also knew that any attempt to convince him that the Army was "now just like any other job, only in uniform" must be fundamentally false.

At this stage of impasse, the opinions of regimental officers were invited. Apart from a few eccentricities (such as the ironic proposal to empty the prisons), we were generally agreed that the government must do one of two things: Either it must employ a strictly "mercenary" army, i.e. pay the very high sums which would be necessary to overcome people's distaste for military discipline; or it must keep National Service going indefinitely, and point out to the country that this was surely a debt that youth must pay in return for the benefits and security it now enjoyed. But both our suggestions were, as we had expected, unacceptable. The Exchequer declined to pay a really generous wage and the country would not tolerate that conscription should continue. Indeed, the authorities began to show rancor. We officers, they said, who had made such futile suggestions, were in any case to blame for the situation. If we showed a better example, both inside barracks and out, if we convinced people by our bearing and attitudes that the Army was a thoroughly good life, then the National Service soldiers under us would fall over themselves to sign on as regulars and fresh recruits would swarm through the barrack gate. Having failed, with all their resources of propaganda, to attract the public at large, the authorities were now pushing the job on to us: We were to undertake, it seemed, individual labors of proselytization among our men —individual in the double sense that we must concentrate, by interviews and personal attentions, on getting individuals to sign up, and that we must also set shining individual examples of enthusiasm, happiness and faith. Meanwhile, the authorities would support us by renewed advertising of the "welfare" type (e.g. "A Colour-Sergeant of thirty years old has x pounds a week, a house with a garden, a shopping center, and full amenities for his family, etc., etc."); and with such assistance we must surely achieve great things. Our results would be carefully scrutinized; let us look to it, and good morning.

Individual reactions to the new individual system were interesting. Major A., who was for the present to co-ordinate our efforts, and who was a very kind and invincibly stupid man, gave us a little talk about how we must not fail the regiment at this perilous juncture, but did not give any precise idea of how we were to proceed. Major B., who was to take over from A. when, in a few weeks' time, he retired, then took us all off for further conference. B. was rich, highly intelligent, and casual in manner; fond of the regiment and loyal to it, he knew how serious the position was, considered the problem insoluble in the terms in which the authorities had set it, but was anxious to do anything he could to improve matters. He therefore made the only possible suggestion—that we should experiment. There was obviously no set formula for so impracticable an assignment; we should just have to try things out, keep one another informed of how they worked—proceed, in fact, by the good old empirical rule of trial and error.

This excellent advice was variously interpreted. Lieutenant C. would do absolutely nothing whatever, on the ground, he said, that the Army was just trying to fob him off with another job—a job for which he would not be paid extra and which was not properly his. It wasn't up to him to dictate their futures to his men. If they liked the Army enough, then they would sign on for regular service; if not they wouldn't, and he didn't blame them. Captain D., with more temperance and subtlety, expressed much the same view. It was all, he said, a matter of *fact*. Life in our regiment had its ups and downs, but was on the whole representative of the Army. The men should therefore be allowed to see and judge it for themselves and to make their decisions accordingly; to try to interpret to them what they saw, or to try to "rig" what they saw so that they should reach a favorable interpretation, was propaganda—it was dishonest and unfair. He would have no part in it; nor would he go about breathing false zeal for his profession: He felt as he did about the Army (affectionate and skeptical) and he did not mind who knew it. If a man came to him for details of "signing on" he would provide them; he was not going to tout the forms around like a salesman.

The newly joined and endearing Second Lieutenant E. ran through a gamut of ideas. First of all, he was inspired by an eighteenth-century recruiting notice which he had seen quoted somewhere and which invited "lusty lads" to partake in a campaign "which will be one long party of pleasure." "We'll drub up King George's enemies," said this infamous document, "then we'll settle to the wine and the women. Come with the glorious ——th, my lads, and see what Fortune brings you." Inflamed by this pronouncement, E. went around encouraging his men to think that a soldier's life was one long picaresque dream of wayside taverns and willing wenches. They had the good sense not to believe him and some of them, being respectable boys, were rather shocked. E.'s efforts were soon in danger of creating scandal, and he was invited to find a more reputable approach.

The next line he hit upon was appeal to male vanity. One of the reasons, he argued, why so many regular recruits went to the Guards was that they were offered a magnificent uniform. People would endure a great deal if they were allowed to wear a scarlet coat. Unfortunately no one in the K.S.L.I. had worn a scarlet coat since 1914, full dress having been long obsolete for the humbler regiments. Never mind, said E.: the thing to do was to whip up romantic feeling for the new Number One Dress with which all regulars were now being issued. Since this consisted of a green coat over blue trousers—a combination which was neither seemly on the one hand nor startling on the other—his work was going to be cut out; and from the day that someone was mistaken for a policeman his failure was assured.

Very well, said E., gritting his teeth. The trouble was that our modern uniforms had no traditional appeal. The thing to do was to emphasize tradition in some other way, to *make* people understand what a privilege it was to belong to a regiment with such a history as ours. He therefore instituted a series of lectures on regimental history. The men enjoyed these, because they happened in a warm room during parade hours, and because the history itself was interesting and at times spectacular; but the recruiting rate stayed as low as ever. When asked if Mr. E.'s lectures did not make them want to remain in the Army, the National Servicemen replied that John Wayne's cowboy films, enjoyable as they were, did not make them want to become cowboys.

If E.'s appeal to pleasure and romance was a flop, an even greater one was Lieutenant F.'s appeal to sober truth. F., a man of some dullness, reckoned that it was his duty to explain to the men the full details of the benefits, pay and prospects offered to those who took on regular engagements. He prepared columns of figures and he gave a long talk rather in the tone of current Army Council advertisements (". . . increases to x shilling a day for substantive corporals of twenty-five . . . gratuities . . . amenities . . . pensions . . ." and so forth); but having outlined the advantages, he was compelled, as a man of integrity, to point out the snags. It must be clearly understood, he remarked, that however snug a soldier might make himself in the new Army, he was liable to be uprooted at a moment's notice; this had never altered and never could—there was no remedy and no appeal against it. And secondly, he felt bound to point out from his own experience that the Army Council played a pretty sharp game; they did not exactly cheat, but they observed the letter and not the apparent spirit of their own instructions, and would always wriggle out of an obligation if they could. Indeed, said F. bitterly, all instructions which promised benefits had subtle means of disqualification built into them: One should never accept an Army Council offer without getting it vetted by a lawyer—and even he might be beaten by some carefully camouflaged piece of tiny print. By the time F. had finished his talk, he had ensured that no man in his platoon would dream of signing on, even though he were offered a thousand-pound bounty in gold by Her Majesty in person.

So our recruiting campaign was, to say the least, ineffective. It was really a double defeat for gentility. For the officers who had conducted it, being honest men, had eschewed deceit and offered only that inducement which they felt was justified by the facts (even Second Lieutenant E.'s talk of drink and women, the product of an overheated imagination, was sincere in its way). The only reward of this straight dealing had been outright failure. In the second place, insofar as their appeal had been based on traditional values (e.g. E.'s attempt to interest his men in the history of the regiment) it had gone unheeded. The men's point of view was absolutely clear: What they wanted was an ordinary civilian boss who, being subject to a mechanism of bargaining and restraint, could be seen as their own equal save for certain purely technical purposes; they refused to be subjected, for twenty-four hours a day, to officers who exercised an arbitrary authority by right of superior, or theoretically superior, qualities. The men were not quite sure whether these qualities were meant to be moral, professional or social; they suspected (more or less rightly) that they were an un-easy mixture of all three. But whatever they were, they wanted nothing to do with them; for the National Serviceman of the fifties the gentleman and his pretensions were relevant only to the past.

And so the months went by, and late in 1957, as I have told earlier in this book, my gambling debts caught up with me and compelled me to resign. I was kindly treated in a dire and discreditable emergency; and for this reason alone I should have remembered the K.S.L.I. with affection. But there are other reasons. It was, when all is said, a friendly, loyal, and rather dotty regiment, tolerant in its demands and moderate in its aspirations. Both the officers and the men were fundamentally decent people; there was little in the way of corruption, self-seeking or malice; judgments and punishments were charitable and few. But none of this need prevent me saying that here, as in the rest of the Army, there prevailed a sense of decline and even of impending collapse, for in their hearts the soldiers no longer accepted the type of authority set over them; and although circumstances might from time to time restore officers to their old and unquestioned status, such circumstances were rare, artificial and brief.

4

MORALS À LA MODE

IF THE PREVIOUS CHAPTER SHOWS that the gentleman is still capable, in certain situations, of regaining his quondam moral authority, the simple incident which I shall now relate is far more typical of the attitudes which in these days he may be expected to adopt. These are attitudes which indicate a definite acceptance of his fall in status, a final recognition that no one will ever again look to him for example or advice. It is as though the gentleman, having been condemned for his own excellence and realizing that any further display of it will be futile or even dangerous, has deliberately fallen in with the debased standards of the age and is perversely determined to promote his own particular varieties of debasement. But however this may be, I now invite the reader to consider the degree of moral and social decay which is implied by the attitudes and actions of the "gentlefolk" who figure in the following story.

Some years ago now, a friend of mine became engaged to a debutante. My friend, whom we shall call Henry, had been a National Service Officer in the Rifle Brigade, had then read history at Cambridge with some success, and had since been employed by a well-known advertising firm; he was quickwitted, presentable, had a little money of his own apart from his generous salary, and so had been welcome at most of the important dances during the two summers he had been in London. His fiancée was three years younger, being just twenty-two; she would bring an annual income of over £2,000 to the altar with her; she was, by debutante standards, liberal and even intellectual in her tastes; she was a well-built girl with fine features, given neither to simpering nor to whining; and all in all, it was felt, my friend could hardly have done better for himself.

On April 5 the marriage was announced for July 10; but on May 2 a notice appeared saying that the marriage would not now take place. This occasioned some surprise, and since I knew Henry well enough to do so I asked him point-blank what had happened.

"She refused to sleep with me before we were married," he said.

"Why?"

"She said she was a Christian and that Christian morality forbade it."

Further inquiry elicited that he had always known she was a Christian but had thought she would be fairly easy in interpreting the more outmoded of Christian precepts. He had wanted to sleep with her straight away, partly because—well, because—and partly because he was anxious to find out about her sexual tastes and capacities as soon as possible rather than spoil the early days of their marriage with false starts. This, as he pointed out, was now common practice among the most respectable of engaged couples.

Even so, I said, in the face of so desirable a match, not to mention the love he presumably bore the girl, could he not let her have her own way?

He had nearly done so, he replied, but had finally balked for two reasons. The lesser of these was that her refusal was an immediate and practical threat to their present happiness. But far more significant than this was the fact that she was in principle prepared and even determined to put a moral scruple before the joint and manifest good of the pair of them. (These days, he added, it could hardly even be called a moral scruple—it was a superstitious one.) Now he was not prepared, Henry said, to spend his life with a woman who put dogmatic injunctions, Christian or otherwise, before the demands of reason and happiness. He had not, when he engaged himself, expected her to take up such stern attitudes (her conversation and bearing had implied the very reverse), and since she was now doing so he could not and would not marry her, and that must be that. He himself had put the notice of cancellation in the *Times*, having first warned his fiancée he would do so.

Unfortunately, however, neither the girl nor her family (whom we will call Balliston) were disposed to take the same view. Sorry as she might be not to fall in with her lover's plans, Carol Balliston nevertheless felt that her refusal did not justify his desertion. He had asked her, whom he knew to be a Christian of good family, to marry him; he could not impose subsequent conditions. As for her "good family," they were outraged. Being worldly people of nearly two generations' upper upper-class standing (ample country estate purchased from deceased father's gains on Lloyd's, mother of sound county origin, two older brothers who had gone straight from Harrow to the City and were themselves underwriters as their father had been), they saw the matter less in terms of morality than as a direct affront to themselves, their possessions and their status. The eldest brother, as head of the family, now called on Henry to make this displeasure plain.

Why, Rufus Balliston wanted to know, had Henry put a notice in the *Times* without telling him?

He had told Carol, Henry said.

But what about her family?

He had been engaged to Carol, not to her family.

But who other than Carol's family, said Rufus Balliston, had been going to provide her very generous marriage settlement? They were intimately concerned in the affair. That a contract should be broken was bad enough, but that Henry, by rejecting Carol, should repudiate the entire Balliston family was much worse. Did Henry not understand that the insult was intolerable? And apart from all this, Carol was deeply wounded; as her eldest brother he must put things right for her.

The last part of this speech, with its element of appeal, had some effect on Henry. Rufus must realize, he said, that the last thing he wanted to do was to hurt Carol, and that he was deeply disappointed at the way things had turned out. But in view of certain traits which he had now detected in her character, he was convinced they could not be happy. Surely Rufus did not want his sister unhappily married?

No, said Rufus, but these things were always dependent on trial and error and mutual allowances. If only Henry would give it time, no doubt Carol and he could adjust themselves to a satisfactory way of life.

Henry thought not.

Very well. If Henry would not make amends, then action must be taken.

What action? Did the Ballistons propose to sue?

No, said Rufus, he did not propose to make his family ridiculous in that way. But he would go and have a word with Henry's employer, a Mr. David Cohen who was an old friend of his father's, and express the Ballistons' distress and resentment.

Was Rufus trying to pressure him? asked Henry.

Certainly not. Just trying to make him see things in a sensible way. . . .

Mr. David Cohen was the son of a Jewish-Latvian immigrant

who had built up a small tailoring business at the cost of his health and his eyesight but had enjoyed the satisfaction of sending the young David to a small public school and thence to Oxford. During the Great War David Cohen had served with great bravery in the ranks of a distinguished infantry regiment and was subsequently commissioned in the field, the first Jew, it was thought, who had ever held commissioned rank in the regiment. Seeing the trend of the age earlier than most people, he had switched his resources (his father now being dead) from tailoring to advertising in the late twenties and had since prospered greatly. Memories of Oxford and of the Officers' Mess, and friends who had remained to him from both, made him gratefully and in many ways stubbornly English; but although he had long ceased to be an orthodox adherent of the Jewish religion, he was still consciously proud of his people and their historic struggle for righteousness, so that when the time came he had married a Jewess (a wealthy one for good measure) and had never forgotten the grandeur of his moral inheritance.

Faced, then, with Rufus Balliston's complaints about Henry's behavior, David Cohen applied conventional English standards oddly mixed with residual Jewish ones. In principle, he agreed, no man should go back on a promise of marriage; furthermore, family loyalty and solidarity required that something be done about it. He, Cohen, had fought with Rufus' father in the trenches and would be glad to be of help if he could be. Just what did Rufus propose to do?

Rufus was hoping, he said, that Cohen, as Henry's employer, could persuade Henry to see sense and to behave . . . correctly.

At this stage Cohen grew grave.

Insofar, he said, as he was Henry's friend, he could advise him—*advise* him—where he thought his duty lay. But he could not command Henry, who was an intelligent and adult man and no doubt had important reasons of his own; and he could not, as his employer, bring any kind of pressure to bear. (He might have been able to had Henry himself been Jewish, but that was not the case.) As a subordinate, Henry gave satisfaction and more, and it was not up to Cohen to supervise his private affairs—unless and until these gave such open scandal that Henry's connection with the firm became harmful to it. After all, this sort of thing, much as he himself disliked it, was now happening among Gentiles every day of the week; for them it no longer had connotations of disgrace. Still, he had known Henry's father as well as Rufus', he had known Henry since he was a boy, and he would see what he could do.

After Rufus left Henry was summoned. Speaking as a father, and partly as a patriarch, Cohen pointed out how wounding Henry's decision must have been to Carol Balliston and her family, and how justified Rufus was in trying to set matters to rights. Henry, respecting the old man and wishing to stand well with him, gave a frank account of his motives. As the child of his age, he said, and as the kind of person he was, he could not have his married life dominated by the excessive religious sensibility of his wife. He could, of course, hold to his bargain with Carol and then, if they continued to disagree over her principles and scruples, seek solace elsewhere—an excellent worldly arrangement by which husband and wife each went their own way. But such an arrangement required mutual forbearance, and to judge from her performance hitherto Carol would not be forbearing and would be made acutely unhappy by his laxity. In all the circumstances it was best to wind the matter up. He had spoken too soon, he admitted, but then Carol herself had been partly to blame for this. To put it crudely, she had adopted a "come-hither" look which promised greater tolerance than she in fact possessed. He was not going to be caught like that.

In short, said Cohen, Henry was going to put his presumptive personal happiness before his promise to Carol.

He only, said Henry, asked a small thing of her. If she was ready to sleep with him now, then he would marry her as planned.

Cohen, the English father and the Jewish patriarch, was temporarily outraged. It was not a small thing; a wife should go to her husband an untouched virgin; it was part of the bargain whereby the husband took her off her parents' hands; it was commanded in the Law that—but here he remembered himself in time and asked Henry whether a decent Englishman could really think so lightly of chastity.

He liked to know where he *stood,* said Henry. As far as he could see, sex was important in marriage, and it was therefore absurd to go into battle, as it were, without previous reconnaissance.

But by this time it was plain that on this topic they would find no common ground. Both of them had a plausible case, but their terms of reference were a thousand miles apart. So Cohen simply said that he hoped Henry would reconsider his attitude, that in any case this could make no difference to his position in the firm, and wished him a good morning.

The next intervention was on the part of a friend of Henry's called Julian Fane. This was a well-meaning and quietly spoken ex-regular officer of the Royal Navy who had decided to leave the service after the war and so, though several years older than Henry, had been his contemporary at Cambridge. For some reason Fane saw himself as being *in loco patris* to Henry and was constantly appearing on the scene, if not in time to curb Henry's recklessness, at any rate soon enough to help clear up the mess. Like the Balliston brothers he worked at Lloyd's, so that although Henry had not yet consulted him about the current imbroglio he had picked up enough gossip to conclude that something was amiss. He therefore presented himself in Henry's flat one evening and, without apology, demanded to hear what was going on. Glad of a prospective ally, Henry told him in full. But Julian Fane, though ultimately on Henry's side in everything, had always felt in his naval way that Henry needed a certain amount of discipline for his own good; and he also had old-fashioned ideas about chivalry to women. Himself given to rather Edwardian affairs with actresses and the wives of absent friends, he was nevertheless scrupulous in his conduct of these; so that it was a commonplace among his friends that Julian Fane behaved with more grace and credit within a framework of adultery than did almost any husband within that of marriage. Julian, in fact, had very strict rules which he conceived that Henry had now violated, and he took him to task accordingly.

In no circumstances, said Julian, could one break one's promise to a woman. Only with the lady's agreement could an engagement

be broken off, and in this case Henry had not secured that agreement.

That was all very well, Henry replied, but Julian, for all his
Arthurian talk, would be the last person to saddle himself for life
with a woman who was going to make him unhappy.

Julian would not have spoken until he was sure.

Well, Henry had made that mistake, and now he had found it
out and had gone back on his promise, and although he would do
anything within reason to make reparation he would not re-engage
himself except on his terms—and these Carol had steadfastly refused
to meet. So what did Julian suggest?

Julian said, rather pompously, that his education had not
equipped him to prescribe for broken faith. But he would undertake to go to Carol as a sort of ambassador from Henry and explain
as kindly and convincingly as possible that Henry had really acted
in all sincerity, was doing what he thought was best for everyone,
and had not simply been amusing himself at Carol's expense. He
would also, Julian said, do his best to stop Rufus Balliston making
a nuisance of himself, and would report back to Henry in a few
days. With that he took his leave, whereupon Henry rang up a
seventeen-year-old student in R.A.D.A., who had been his mistress
up to the time of his engagement, and asked her out to dinner.

So he had given up the idea of marriage? said Henry's student,
lashing into a double portion of *foie gras*.

This marriage, said Henry, yes.

And what about the poor girl he had jilted?

It was all for her own good, and she'd get over it.

Well, if Henry said so . . . the girl said, applying herself to a
lobster cooked in white wine and truffles. And now, she supposed,
Henry would be wanting to sleep with *her* again.

Yes.

Well, she didn't mind if he did, on the whole. She only had one
other boy friend at the moment. He was a sweet thing—American
and quite rich—but he was no good at all in bed. So if it was all
right with Henry, she would have her other friend in the afternoon

sometimes, and keep the nights for him. And she carefully cut the breasts from a woodcock which had been flared in brandy.

It seemed, Henry said, a very satisfactory arrangement.

So they went and giggled at a nude show together, and then went home to bed.

Meanwhile, Julian Fane's exercise in diplomacy was not turning out well. He had called at the Balliston household to find Carol out and Rufus in; so he had immediately bearded Rufus and said straight out that since Henry and the Balliston family were not at all suited to each other it was a good job things had turned out as they had.

Very likely, said Rufus; but he could not forget the insulting way in which Henry had managed it all.

Henry meant no harm, said Julian; this was the way things were done nowadays, even if Rufus and he himself did not think much of it.

If in this style Julian managed in some part to mollify Rufus, it was only to find, when Carol came in, that she was going to be a much tougher proposition than her brother. She was as hard as nails.

She was not, she said, going to listen to any excuses on Henry's behalf. He had proposed to her in proper form, everything had been arranged; that she had then found herself unable to meet his wishes in some particular (though she would have liked to have done so had it been possible) was no justification for his betrayal. Julian must understand that she loved Henry and was anxious, in general, to be married and to have children. She could not dictate to her heart as easily as Henry apparently could, so it would now be some time before she recovered and was able to look around once more with a view to marriage. This did not suit her at all; indeed it was intolerable. It was Henry's duty to marry her and marry her he must. If he didn't, then whatever Rufus said about making fools of themselves she would sue Henry herself.

Julian had not at all bargained for this. Not knowing Carol very well, he had seen himself in the role of comforter and had come with two or three spare handkerchiefs. He was consequently shocked at so unfeminine an exhibition; but pulling himself together, he pointed out that action such as she proposed would only make for bad blood and would achieve nothing. Never mind, said Carol; it would in some sort compensate for the unhappiness she had sustained and, what was more, *right* was on her side.

And so when Julian went to report all this to Henry he sympathized with his friend much more than he had done. Henry had a good point—life with anyone so stubborn and uncompromising would be impossible. But what was to be done? The problem was discussed over a dinner at which the R.A.D.A. girl was present.

"So," said Henry, "Carol's going to sue?"

"Yes," said Julian.

"Bitch," said the R.A.D.A. girl.

"This will upset Davie Cohen."

"It will be very distasteful."

"Slut," said the R.A.D.A. girl, taking a very large helping of *pommes lyonnaises.*

"What can we do?"

"Find her another man," said the R.A.D.A. girl, "and quickly."

"You might have something there," said Henry.

"But she says," pursued Julian, "that she cannot contemplate a change of heart for a long time."

"Balls," said the R.A.D.A. girl, "you find her someone as good as Henry, and she'll eat him up. Literally, I wouldn't wonder. It's only a question of giving her proper value."

And at least, as they all agreed, it was worth a try.

So the R.A.D.A. girl produced for their inspection the "other boy friend" of whom she had told Henry some evenings before. "Since she won't sleep with anyone till she's married, she won't find out how useless he is until too late," the R.A.D.A. girl had remarked. Externally the young American whom she presented to them was everything that could be desired. He had originally come to England on an exchange fellowship and was now spending a year at the London School of Economics before returning to New York to work in his father's publishing firm; he was well informed, witty in a rather painstaking way, tall, fair, clean and boyish (yet unmistakably handsome and not just pretty), and he was the soul of kindness and courtesy. And, it appeared, of honor. "He's always asking me to marry him," said the R.A.D.A. girl. "Every time he sleeps with me, in fact. He says that fornication makes him feel guilty. But you can't be married to a great innocent thing like that if your life is in the theater." No more you could, but in every way he was suitable for Carol. It was arranged that Julian, who was slightly shocked but whom they managed to persuade, should give a small dinner party to which both Carol and the American should be invited, the American having been warned beforehand that Carol had recently suffered some unhappiness. This, it was thought, would interest and attract his kindly nature. It did. And his nature attracted Carol: Here was someone who was clever and good and, above all, malleable. The gods were on the side of the schemers. Carol and the American took an instant liking to each other and found much mutual pleasure in each other's probity (the American far more enjoyed *not being allowed* to sleep with her than he would have enjoyed her actual favors). They were seen together behaving fondly but rather severly in theaters, restaurants and exhibitions; and within two months of meeting they were engaged.

So Henry was let off, and Carol found a husband, and the American found what he had always no doubt wanted—a woman to boss him about, to relieve his guilt by punishing him. Julian Fane was uneasily satisfied that all wrongs had been more or less righted; and the R.A.D.A. girl ate many lavish dinners with Henry and passed many happy nights in his flat. Things, you might say, could have fallen out a lot worse. And yet consider, for a moment, the impoverished motives behind this wholly typical intrigue. Henry, to begin with, simply wanted a smart and beneficial marriage with his own way thrown in. Carol wanted to go publicly and with pomp to the altar, and had used a conventional religious response to make herself and her nuptial seem far more important than they really were and, later, to enable her to feel "wronged." Rufus Balliston was concerned only with the insult to his name and property. David Cohen, it is true, showed a certain moral dignity; but this was uneasily mixed up with archaic Jewish notions of marriage prospects and marriage bargains, and was also considerably qualified by his commercial instincts—which told him that he must not risk the loss of a valuable employee. Julian Fane was prepared to make a stand in the name of chivalry, but could not hold up long against the frivolity of Henry and the earthy good humor of the R.A.D.A. girl; Julian's misgivings, such as they were, belonged to another age and could not survive in the moral climate in which he lived. Finally, the gentle and ethical American ended up, as such people in such surroundings are bound to end up, as the fall guy or scapegoat. Possibly he was quite happy about it, and later possibly not. An inescapable impression remains of innocence having been exploited, of moral scruple having been debased, and of promises having been blown upon and scattered like common dandelions in the rank month of June.

5

ALMA MATER

IN ALL THAT has gone so far, I stand to be charged with having said too much about the gentleman's merits and too little about his defects. I have qualified his snobberies and even applauded his limitations. And yet my whole thesis, in a way, has been an indictment of him, for I have shown—or tried to show—that the special qualities of the gentleman have proved futile in our own time and have amply invited its hostility. True, it may sometimes have seemed that I was trying to indict the age for ruining the gentleman rather than the gentleman for being at odds with the age, and certainly I find much in modern life to detest. But it is no good quarreling with established conditions. The times are what they are, and they might be a great deal worse. Certain inevitable and on the whole desirable social developments have now rendered the gentleman a superfluous nuisance. One may be glad of this or one may be sorry, but either way there is nothing to be done.

Or *is* there nothing to be done? Certainly no amount of mourning or moralizing can bring the gentleman back again, for history has gone too far; yet might it not be possible, might it not even prove essential, to replace him with someone else—someone different but comparable? But why, it will be retorted, should we want to do that? Society has scarcely rid itself of one elite, and here are you hankering after another.

But I am not, as I shall later make plain, proposing an elite; and I only want to put someone in the gentleman's empty place for the very good reason that someone must inherit his function. Democracy or no democracy, there must be rule and administration, and these were the special provinces of the gentleman. At the present moment they are being attended to by those who seem in their various ways to be *technically* qualified. Positions are no longer sought by right of gentle status but by displaying after one's name certain combinations of letters which purport to guarantee certain skills— skills scientific, educational, executive and the rest. All right, you may say, this is a complicated and scientific age, and we must therefore have people of specialized and proven abilities to cope with its problems. I agree most heartily; but the trouble is that while a degree may (or may not) be evidence of professional ability, it can never confer authority in the *wider sense*. For rulers, administrators, educators—even for research workers—some such general authority is essential. At the very least, there will be laboratory assistants to be organized, or hysterical cooks to be pacified when the schoolchildren have spurned their dinners; while at higher levels there will be whole towns and counties to be persuaded, whole nations, perhaps, to be disciplined. It is just this kind of authority, the authority that can soothe the quarrel of the minute or launch the policy of the decade, which once belonged to gentlemen and which is lacking in their successors.

In the gentleman's heyday, technical knowledge was either despised or hired. The gentleman himself seldom had it; very often it wasn't needed; and if it was, then an underling would provide it while the gentleman continued to provide the necessary backing of authority. This state of affairs was always questionable and would currently be intolerable. Clearly, those who order our lives should have the highest technical qualifications, and increasingly often they do. But all this will be useless unless they also have that sense of obligation and that power of inspiring trust which together make for true authority. It is of no use to be an agricultural expert unless you can get the farmer to follow your advice; it is no good knowing every valve in the engine of a tank unless you can also make your soldiers climb into it and drive it onto the battlefield; it is futile to have mastered the latest pediatric theories and to be received by a class of ten-year-olds with contempt. The point is clear. And it is equally clear that this overall and binding authority to which I refer is at present hardly anywhere to be seen.

Everywhere there are instances, petty, laughable or grave, of its lack. A hotel manager, hung about with diplomats, cannot get his maids to dust the bedrooms properly. The men of a famous regiment burn down the colonel's tent and threaten worse unless they are instantly promised a luxurious canteen and a swimming pool. A teen-age girl goes to school togged up like a whore and refuses, with her parents' support, to dress more suitably the next day. A small boy is mildly cuffed for being a nuisance, and a case for assault comes before the local magistrates. A colonial servant, well versed in the law, cannot keep rudimentary order in his court. A young doctor dares not accuse a malingerer and prescribes colored water for him instead. A single worker conceives a trivial grievance, and a contract worth millions is lost or broken. Why multiply examples? There is one on every page of today's paper, as there was yesterday and will be tomorrow. What has happened is very plain: Just as technical standards have risen so has authority declined. The new rulers are without the one quality which the gentleman, for all his ignorance and narrowness, of his very nature possessed: self-reliance.

What I shall try to do in this chapter is *not* to render a blueprint for a new elite, but simply to suggest a way of stiffening, of priming with the necessary minimum of confidence and authority, those who have important positions among us. In many ways it is suitable that democratic leaders and administrators should be shy of asserting themselves, and certainly no return is possible to the more direct and brutal of the methods which the gentleman sometimes employed. Equally, the gentleman often used methods which, though based in authority, displayed understanding and courtesy. Let us consider, then, whether some such methods might not be compatible with the new manners of democracy, and whether even equality might not admit of some distinction.

I shall now describe a situation in which it seems to me that something of what I advocate was achieved.

When I arrived, in 1948, at King's College, Cambridge, I already knew that it was a friendly and easygoing institution, with a tradition of eccentricity, tolerance, and intellectual integrity, this last being much associated with rational agnosticism. I also knew that it had certain aesthetic advantages. It boasted an unrivaled choir (to which even an agnostic might listen for his pleasure); it had two of the finest buildings in Europe; and one might look, down river from the college bridge, at one of the most beautiful and tranquil views in the world. With all this, there were many persons living in the college who added personal charm to high attainments; and as for the undergraduates, they were, on the whole, well mannered and modest, having apparently shed any schoolboy tendencies to interfere with other people in the cause of morality or team games.

This much I knew, one way and the other, before ever I came up. What I had not been prepared for was the great trouble taken by even the most distinguished Fellows to mix with undergraduates on terms of friendship and equality. That the dons would be pleasant to us, that they would occasionally ask us to meals, offer advice or lend us money, I had foreseen. But a degree of intimacy whereby they make us free of their personal lives, lent their closest support to all our interests (of whatever kind), shared our gossip and even got drunk in our company—this I had not looked for. Nor were things at all the same in other colleges, the members of which regarded us with mistrust and deposed that our way of life must be at best frivolous and at worst totally ruinous to work and discipline. And here, indeed, is the crux of the matter. For despite the understandable suspicion of outsiders, despite our own freedom of manners, despite the drinking and the chatter and the license, authority did in truth prevail among us.

Authority. Thus far we might go and no farther. In the last resort we must do, and were content to do, what we were told. There were certain requirements, in the interest of good order and sound learning, to which we must be subject. You might call a don by his first name, drink with him and exchange scurrilous information until the dawn; but if he threw back a careless exercise, or refused you permission to go away for the weekend, then you must submit. Authority. You might complain, you might reason or cajole, but you might not disobey. Your morals might be considered your own affair, you might be told personally by a senior college official of the best ways of climbing in or out, you might express the most vigorous contempt for God and all His works; but if you openly endangered good order (by embracing the girls from Girton in broad daylight, being rude to a porter who caught you climbing in, or making a rumpus in the college chapel), then you had gone too far and must accept the punishment which, without malice, would be handed out to you. Again, if we abused our opportunities as scholars, rejected our tutors' advice or neglected their assignments, we were wasting everybody's time and had better go. Authority. It was accepted by all of us. The Junior Dean would offer a glass of gin or announce that you were to be rusticated in the same friendly tone of voice. One accepted the sentence as one might accept any statement of fact from a trusted equal. This was so, one told oneself; there could be no question of denying or resenting something so self-evidently true.

What was the secret of this authority—this amiable, equable, effortless control? Odd though it may seem, I think one part of it was sheer learning. We were dealing with learned men. Not only did we respect them as such, but we also knew that they were daily accustomed to seek out and sift evidence, to apply to it the processes of comparison and logic, and to publish, after careful testing, conclusions which they believed to be the truth. It therefore seemed probable that they would use the same objective methods when handling our affairs. Their decisions, though possibly softened by friendship after they were reached, would not, in the making, be warped by prejudice; there would be something *absolute* about them, for they would be stamped with the hallmark of intellect. And for this very reason, such decisions would then be made known with complete *frankness*—which was the second element behind the Fellows' authority. Since they were dealing in truth and logic, it was unthinkable that they should conceal or be evasive about their findings. If they found that you were a fraud they told you so—openly and without ill will. It was just another established fact which went to make up the account; facts were what they were and must be faced, because if you ignored them you made a wrong reckoning and reached the wrong result.

Along with learning and frankness came skepticism. This operated in two ways. No one would believe anything until it was actually proved; and secondly, even if it should be proved people remained alert for fresh evidence, having often enough in their lives seen a famous theory collapse overnight because of a scrap of parchment or a frivolous experiment. This meant that they refused to accept supernaturally "revealed" truth or any dogmatic creed, and that they therefore rejected individual judgments that were based on such a creed. It also meant that despite the care and integrity with which they reached their decisions, and despite the respect which we accorded those decisions, they themselves were wary of regarding them as final. For in any case whatever, and over and above all, they were mindful of the most important truth of the lot —that to be human is to be fallible.

From all of which it followed that they were endlessly tolerant. Tolerance was perhaps the most powerful ingredient in their authority. They were tolerant of anything and anybody. Had they not read their history books? There was ample precedent in these for anything which could possibly occur inside the college and for a great deal more besides. This was not to say that all these things could be *allowed*—arson and murder at least must be discouraged.

But even as they punished or expelled a grave offender, they made
it clear that they had nothing against him personally—that they entirely understood why he had (say) cudgeled the Senior Fellow
with a niblick, but just could not suffer someone who was given to
such practice to remain. He would be glad to know that the old
gentleman was off the danger list, they all wished him luck in the
forthcoming trial, and now, my dear boy, good morning. . . . There
were times when the Fellows of King's reminded one of Sir Pitt
Crawley, who would crack a joke with a man from the bench in
the very act of having him transported. But Sir Pitt's tolerance came
from indifference, theirs from knowledge and reason; it was at once
massive and flexible, as impenetrable as concrete, as enveloping as
a cloud.

Learning, frankness, skepticism, tolerance. By these means did the
Fellows of King's exercise authority from a deliberately assumed
position of equality. I myself was involved in an affair which, trivial
in itself, gives a very fair notion of their methods.

At the end of my second year I found myself, not for the first
time, quite incapable of paying my college bill. I was therefore told
that since I persisted in inconveniencing other people I must expect
to be inconvenienced myself: If I had not discharged the debt by
1 September, then I would be ejected from my Scholar's rooms in
college and sent out to lodge in a suburb of the town. Fairly spoken;
and the more fairly as the speaker then found me a well-paid vaca-
tion job which should have enabled me to clear my debt with ease.
But I drank my earnings (hoping, and failing, to borrow the necessary sum at the last minute) and was duly removed to the suburbs
the following October.

I had many friends who lived in college, my interests, social and
otherwise, centered on it; and so I was sorely put out. Some of the
best things in King's happened after midnight—by which time I was
meant to be back in my lodgings. Finding, however, that my new
landlady was somewhat lax—she was prepared to leave the front
door unlocked and not to bother about when I came and went—I
was able to arrive at a tolerable *modus vivendi*. The basis of this
was that when anything came up to keep me late in college, rather

than climb out of it in the small hours and bicycle two miles (drunk) to my digs, I simply slept the night in one of the college guest rooms. In the morning I would shave and breakfast in a friend's room, and was right on the spot to begin the business and pleasure of the new day.

But while this nomadic form of life suited and amused me, it gave no satisfaction to bedmakers or porters. Rooms which should have been ready for guests were found to have been used and abused the night before (no one as yet knew by whom) and a last-minute rush was necessary to clean them up. Distinguished visitors were either awakened when I made my reconnaissance or arrived to find me already asleep in their beds. Although I never went as far as a friend of mine, who was sick in the bath of a visiting bishop and neglected to wipe up the mess, cumulatively I must have caused far more discomfort and anguish. And so the weeks passed and the menace of the Unknown Sleeper grew.

But when the summer came, and with it a marked increase in entertainments, I went too far. For four days on end I haunted the college, and finally I was found, at 11 A.M. on a Saturday, sleeping in a bed that was to be occupied that night by an Indian professor of sociology. I was reported to and summoned by the Dean in office, who knew me quite well, as he taught me Ancient Philosophy. First of all he gave me a glass of sherry; then he commented on an essay I had just sent in; finally, and almost as a second thought, he advised me to spend a pleasant evening since he proposed, as from the next day, to gate me for three weeks. This meant that every evening for the next three weeks I must be in my suburban lodgings by 9 P.M. and not stir abroad until the following morning.

"Why?" I said.

"For sleeping in college guest rooms without first booking them. You have given great trouble and have also avoided the expense of paying for your accommodation."

This was especially apt. I was being punished, not for my grave breach of regulations in being absent at night from my digs, but for occupying guest rooms without proper warning or acknowledgment. Suave good sense could go no farther.

"But," I said, "three weeks, especially in the summer, is a very long time. If I were being gated inside the college, the punishment would be negligible. But to be gated outside it and at the end of the Milton Road . . ."

It was, the Dean agreed, a great pity, and no doubt it would be very disagreeable. One must look on the bright side, of course; I could now devote my evenings to preparing for my papers in Ancient Philosophy. By the way, if I broke my gating he would have to send me down for good. . . . This amiable conversation continued, rather as though we were discussing the mild misfortunes of a common friend, until once again he wished me a pleasant evening and excused himself as he had work.

There followed three weeks of misery, which was only dissipated on the evenings when loyal friends made the dreary trek up the Milton Road to see me.

"Poor Simon," said a lecturer in English.

"I do think it's rather hard."

"But you were rather naughty. And it's not for ever. And of course *if* you took it into your head to break out one of these nights, that would be the last we should ever see of you here—which would make some of us, at least, *quite* sorry."

This was the second time that what was in fact a grim warning had been casually yet clearly conveyed, without hectoring and as in the course of mere friendly conversation. If it was impossible to misunderstand the threat, it was also impossible to resent it. Here surely was the face of authority, and also a face one must accept and even love. One could tell the face it was being rather harsh, whereupon it would smile, sympathize, and possibly agree; but it was inconceivable that one should defy the face, if only because it was entirely innocent of vindictiveness.

The whole matter ended typically enough. When my sentence was nearly done, I asked for a remission of three days as I wished to go to a party in London. It was to be a gay and significant party, as it would be attended by many of my friends and by several persons of distinction whom I was anxious to meet. I put my request to the Dean, and was referred to the Tutor himself, as whose agent the Dean had been acting throughout. The Tutor being away for the day, I sent in my request in writing and visited him in person the next morning. He remarked that he was quite glad to see me, as he had been wanting to comment on an article of mine which had just appeared in the *Cambridge Review*.

"Rather cheap on the whole," he said, after offering several pertinent criticisms, "but I shall look forward to seeing more. . . . And by the way I'm so sorry you are prevented from going to London tomorrow. You would have enjoyed meeting X—and Y—, but I dare say there'll be other chances. . . ."

There was no more to be said. He had spoken in the tones of a dove and with the effect of a Regimental Sergeant-Major.

Such, then, was the authority, unquestioned and unresented, which obtained in King's College. I now ask myself whether something of the kind, more generally applied, might not replace the vanished gentleman's authority in the guidance and government of the nation.

I do not advocate the rule of an elite, still less am I so absurd as to propose government by juntas of Kingsmen. All I am saying is that the modified type of authority which I have tried to describe above could be valuable in our affairs. At present our administrators are without true authority; the effects of this are daily more apparent and daily more likely to involve us in yet another colossal fiasco such as we saw at the time of Suez. Since we can no longer tolerate rule *de haut en bas*, *i.e.* rule based on superiority, what more reasonable than that we should seek to develop some form of *authority between equals*, such as I have illustrated here?

In its essence, this authority is a refined and, one might say, a democratized version of that once exercised by the traditional gentleman. It has the same imperious regard for obligation, loyalty and truth, the same distrust of enthusiasm and bigotry, and, although it pays no regard to the petty details of personal morality, the same ultimate moral purpose. The difference is that it does not condescend nor does it conceive of itself as operating by social right. It operates between equals by mutual consent and in order to uphold the common good. In some ways it resembles charity—it vaunteth not itself and is not puffed up, it suffereth long and is kind. Unlike charity, however, it ministers as much to human strength as to human weakness; for it assumes that we are all capable of looking facts in the face and accepting them for what they are.

And this, of course, is just where it would likely be brought down. For the truth is that very few people can endure to look at facts unless these have been carefully arranged for them first. (I have remarked elsewhere in this essay on democratic methods of begging questions and blinking facts.) King's College was a small society in which most people were intelligent and well disposed; they were therefore prepared to face facts and to accept, from acknowledged equals, an authority based on facts. "You have made a mistake; if you want your work to be any good you must now go away and correct it." This sort of remark, a reasonable proposition in the light of fact which was made as by one friend to another, was typical of the everyday practice which worked so well. But could it work in a wider field? Most people these days object to being told of their mistakes, even by their own equals; for in pointing out another's failure, they think, lies an implicit denial of equality. Jacques Barzun (in *The House of Intellect*) tells of a student who, on being informed that his writing was illegible, retorted, "It's *my* writing, isn't it?" We all have our own way of doing things, that is to say, and in a democracy no one way can be better than another. If even students can take this line, what hope is there for the public at large?

But such questions must lie beyond my present scope, which is to record and to suggest, not to reform. This book has dealt with a code which once conferred a certain authority upon certain people —people who, for all their faults, often used this authority to selfless and noble ends. I have described here how the climate of our time has caused the code to droop and wither, and how the gentleman and his authority have also drooped. In this last chapter I have tentatively suggested that another code, less rigorous, more intellectual, more delicate, might take the place of the gentleman's. It has been, I think, both presumptuous and naïve of me to do so; and in any case I incline to the opinion that even this code, with all its allowance for equality, would inevitably be doomed.

For any authority, however flexible and however enlightened, must in the last resort of all depend upon respect. In King's we were all accounted equals but we were equals who respected one another and based our respect in a proper recognition of individual excellence; and so there could be authority between equals. But in the world at large there is no respect. Or rather, there is so much respect, since anything or anybody at all must now be accorded it, that the word is made meaningless. The most trivial platitudes, the most misleading and sentimental half-truths, the merest nonsense —all must be received with "respect," lest feelings be hurt and "justifiable resentment" aroused. Is the work shoddy? Are the foundations shallow, the supports unseasoned, the bricks carelessly laid? But this, my friend, is the work of free and equal men, and even as the house totters to the ground you must treat the builders with "respect." Fools, knaves, malingerers; the stupid, the incapable, the idle and the vicious; the nursers of grievances, the detractors of virtue, the spiteful, the envious, the mediocre and the mean—any and all of these you must "respect." Respect the people, respect their "rights," respect labor and respect its dignity, respect simplicity, respect ignorance, respect superstitious opinion, public morals, minority prejudice and majority hysteria—all these you must and will respect. But one thing you may not respect. Excellence or merit. Because if you respect this, you stand to allow that someone is better than someone else, and that, by current reckoning, is to destroy respect. Respect has been inverted: It is now what the great or gifted man must pay to his average fellows—in return for which they may possibly suffer him to serve them. *Their* respect is reserved for a different purpose—to console and flatter themselves. There can be none to spare for the authority of learning or of practiced tolerance or even of plain fact; still less to spare for that honorable figure of a vanished age—the English Gentleman.

Deal, March 18, 1961

About the Author

Simon Raven is the author of *The Feathers of Death, Brother Cain* and *Doctors Wear Scarlet.*

A reviewer for the *Spectator,* he also contributes regularly to *Punch,* the *London Times Literary Supplement* and *Encounter.* He wrote a much talked about and controversial article for *The Establishment,* a study of England's ruling class, edited by Hugh Thomas.

Of his first book, *The Feathers of Death,* The *Observer* noted that "there is something irresistible about the vigor of his attack." The *Evening News* said that it was "a first novel of outstanding quality, written with passion and comprehension and with a rigid moral sense upholding it." *Newsweek* called his second book, *Brother Cain,* "witty, sophisticated and satiric."